ANGELS AND HEROES

To Mike

Best wishes
Amanda Moreno
15/9/2004

Faugh-a-Ballagh!

Sgt Hugh Alexander Wilson, author of 'Eight months on the spree: the story of a machine gunner with the Royal Irish Fusiliers August 1914 to April 1915'.

ANGELS AND HEROES

THE STORY OF A MACHINE GUNNER WITH THE ROYAL IRISH FUSILIERS AUGUST 1914 TO APRIL 1915

As recorded by
Sergeant Hugh Wilson
(Medaille Militaire)

Compiled by
Amanda Moreno BA
David Truesdale

The Royal Irish Fusiliers Museum

This book is dedicated to the memory of a remarkable soldier
Sergeant Hugh Alexander Wilson, 1886-1947
who served with
1st Battalion Royal Irish Fusiliers, 1902-1916
and to his family, whose generosity has made this book possible

First published in 2004

British Library Cataloguing in Publication Data

A catalogue record for this book is available from the British Library.

ISBN 0 9548383 0 0

Published by

The Royal Irish Fusiliers Museum
Sovereign's House
The Mall
Armagh
Northern Ireland BT61 9DL
028 3752 2911
rylirfusiliermus@aol.com
www.rirfus-mus@freeserve.co.uk

in association with

Silver Link Publishing Ltd
The Trundle
Ringstead Road
Great Addington
Kettering
Northants NN14 4BW
Tel/Fax: 01536 330588
email: sales@nostalgiacollection.com
Website: www.nostalgiacollection.com

Printed and bound in Great Britain

All illustrations are from the Museum's collection or were specially commissioned for this book and are the copyright of the Royal Irish Fusiliers Museum; Arthur J. Clarke; Jan Ballantyne; and William Dobbin.

The maps are from Brigadier Burrowes *The First Battalion, the Faugh-a-Ballaghs in the Great War.*

CONTENTS

ACKNOWLEDGEMENTS

A book can only be written with the help, guidance, advice and patience of many people. If we have forgotten anyone, please accept our apologies and sincere thanks for your contribution. We would like to express our appreciation to the following: Iris Williamson, from the Royal Irish Fusiliers Museum, who enthusiastically took on the task of transcribing Sgt Wilson's diaries; in seeking out answers to the most obscure queries we repeatedly turned to the encyclopaedic knowledge of Cameron Robinson, whose answers were always given gladly, swiftly and with absolute accuracy; and for help regarding vapour trails, Ernie Cromie of the Ulster Aviation Society.

Thanks also to David Orr; John Young, for an insight into the life and career of General H. L. Smith-Dorrien; and Dr Stephen Vallely, for information on nutrition, exhaustion and stress. Sincere thanks to Nicola Clarke for proof-reading and making many valuable suggestions. For taking most of the photographs, proof-reading and editing, credit is due to Arthur Clarke. Thanks also to Jan Ballantyne for taking the photographs at Le Mans. For delving through their archives, the help of Craig McGuicken and Billy Ervine at the Somme Heritage Centre was gratefully appreciated. Many thanks to Will Adams and Mick Sanders at Silver Link Publishing for their enthusiasm and sterling work in producing this book.

Finally, from Amanda, to my parents Sarah and Alex Wilson, there are no words of appreciation fulsome enough to express the debt I owe to them. What I have achieved is as a result of their efforts and support. That I could freely spend time in France researching and writing this book was due to their dedication and hard work in looking after my home life.

Sources

The First Battalion, the Faugh a Ballaghs in the Great War by Brigadier A. R. Burrowes (Gale & Polden, 1929)

Orange Green and Khaki by Tom Johnstone (Gill & McMillan, 1992)

The Retreat from Mons by A. Corbett-Smith (Major RFA) (Cassell & Company Ltd, 1916)

Forgotten Victory by Gary Sheffield (Review, 2001)

Mud, Blood and Poppycock by Gordon Corrigan (Cassell, 2003)

British Butchers and Bunglers of World War Two by John Laffin (Sutton Publishing, 1998)

Are We Listening to the Angels by Robert J. Grant (ARE Press, 2002)

Burke's Medical Dictionary (William A. R. Thompson) (3rd edition, 1981)

The Little Book of War Poems by Nick de Somogyi (Marks & Spencer, 2001)

Before Endeavours Fade by Rose E. B. Coombs MBE (After the Battle, 1983)

A Foreign Field by Ben Macintyre (HarperCollins, 2001)

INTRODUCTION

The phone call that introduced me to the Journal of Sgt Hugh Alexander Wilson came to the Royal Irish Fusiliers Museum one gloomy Monday morning in October 2003. The morning was not gloomy because of the weather; rather it was because the museum had not been able to raise enough funds that weekend to purchase a unique collection of letters written by Captain Kidd of the 5th Battalion Royal Irish Fusiliers. The letters covered his period of service in Gallipoli, Macedonia, Salonika, Palestine and the Western Front.

But, as one door closes, another opens, and through this door I entered the world of one soldier of the British Expeditionary Force. With the simple yet wholly articulate words of Sgt Hugh Wilson, I was privileged to experience the trials and tribulations of a soldier from almost a century ago.

As soon as I read his account of returning to Armagh to collect 300 Reservists mobilised for the 1st Battalion of the Royal Irish Fusiliers, in preparation for the Great War, I knew this Journal had to be published. It seemed a fitting way to mark the 90th anniversary of the start of the First World War and those first chaotic months of fighting, when both Sgt Wilson and the British Army were on a steep learning curve.

Having little experience in the literary world, I approached a good friend and published military historian, David Truesdale, and what follows is a joint effort. However, any mistakes are mine and not his.

From the beginning we accepted that the Journal has occasional grammatical and spelling errors, though these are easily forgiven when you become immersed in the vernacular of the 1914 soldier. Accordingly, we have decided to leave Sgt Wilson's words intact, with any relevant explanations in the footnotes.

To start I have written a brief account of the Regiment and the period leading up to the conflict. This will set the scene for Sgt Wilson's Journal, as it records his actions over the first eight months of the Great War. The achievements of this proud Irish Regiment have echoed down through the years and pervade the actions of each generation that has served – like silent sentinels standing shoulder to shoulder with the men in the trenches. Soldiers have always gleaned courage and comfort from the knowledge that generations of soldiers before them have felt their same fear on the eve of battle.

The Royal Irish Fusiliers was formed in Dublin in 1793, originally as two separate regiments, the 87th and 89th Foot. Both regiments recruited soldiers throughout Ireland, from Armagh to Tipperary, and Gaelic was the first language of most of the soldiers. Their battle cry is also Gaelic, 'Faugh-a-Ballagh', hence their nickname, the Faughs; it translates as 'Clear the Way', and they were the only regiment in the British Army ever to have a Gaelic motto. Throughout this book the Regiment is referred to as either the Faughs, the 1st Battalion or by its full title, the Royal Irish Fusiliers.

The biggest landmark in the history of the Faughs was during the Peninsular War (1808-14). Napoleon's total control of Europe had started to collapse when Spain rebelled and allied with Britain. The British and Spanish armies landed at Tarifa, their aim being to relieve the Spanish force at Cadiz, and the key to the attack was the high ground of Barrosa Ridge, overlooking Cadiz. On 5 March 1811 the British Forces stood on top of the ridge, below them their objective, the city of Cadiz. In between were the advancing French, who outnumbered the British force two to one.

Close to the end of the battle, the Colour Party of the French 8th Demi Brigade was desperately defending the Eagle Standard of its regiment. In the final struggle, Sergeant Patrick Masterson of the 87th saw the Eagle held high, and with his men surged forward to snatch it from the dying French officer. This was the first French Imperial Eagle standard to be captured during the war against Napoleon, and was a huge blow to French morale. The Prince of Wales immediately made Sergeant Masterson a commissioned officer, and conferred the title 'Prince of Wales' Own Irish' on the Faughs. As an indication of the importance of the capture, he also gave the Regiment permission to emblazon the French Eagle on all of its regalia. From that day onwards, 5 March, 'Barrosa Day', has been set aside as a special day of celebration within the Regiment.

I have interspersed Sgt Wilson's Journal with extracts from the war diary of the 1st Battalion of the Royal Irish Fusiliers. In the museum archives we hold many fascinating personal letters and diaries written by 1st Battalion soldiers, and I have included snippets from these where they have added to the story.

The four appendices expand slightly on the background to the Journal. The biographies of Sgt Hugh Wilson and Pte Robert Morrow VC are self-explanatory. David Truesdale carried out extensive research before writing the appendix on the legend of the Angel of Mons. At first glance the Order of Battle of the British Expeditionary Force of August 1914 will appear a bewildering list of regiments and units, but please take a few minutes to read through it, to appreciate the enormous task of organising and controlling such vastly differing units before the days of the 'All Arms' or all Services (Navy, Army and Air Force) approach to warfare. Such a list makes it easier to envisage the 600,000 British soldiers who went to war in 1914 and to realise that for every fighting man there were another three soldiers in a vital supporting role.

I trust that, like me, you will find Sgt Wilson's story very moving and utterly absorbing. After 90 years it stands as a fitting tribute to his memory, and that of his comrades, not only in the Faughs, but to all who served in the British Expeditionary Force of 1914.

1
The start of the Great War

It is a common misconception that the First World War was a needless slaughter in which Britain should never have been involved. That so many lives were lost is certainly a tragedy, but it was a war that Britain was obligated to fight in, had to fight in for her own survival, and had to win at all costs.

It is thanks to military historians like Gary Sheffield and Gordon Corrigan that the myths regarding the way in which the war was fought are gradually dissipating. Once more, allowing the soldiers of the Great War to stand proudly in our memory, as honourable men who fought a justified war and not as the tragic figures, misguided and misled, that they have been made out to be.

Germany was created as a result of the war between France and Prussia in 1870-71, and in 1914, as a nation and Empire, it had existed for just over 40 years. Yet this strongly nationalistic state was a formidable economic power on the world stage. Kaiser Wilhelm II, grandson of Queen Victoria, became Emperor of Germany in 1888, and was determined not to be a puppet Emperor. His imperialistic programme of expansion gained Germany new colonies, created the second most powerful navy in the world (next to Britain) and the largest, best trained and equipped army in the world.

His policies had a purpose. At the Kaiser's behest, first Field Marshal von Moltke then Field Marshal von Schlieffen drew up detailed plans for war in Europe. By 1912 the plans for the invasion of France and Belgium were complete. They were never intended as a contingency or a defence against possible danger to Germany, but a comprehensive strategy for the expansion of Germany.

The Schlieffen Plan was well thought out and prepared. It clearly set out how the German Army would sweep through Belgium, thereby avoiding the French Army and its line of forts on the Franco-German border. Schlieffen calculated that the German Army could defeat France and Belgium before France's ally Russia would have time to mobilise.

While the Kaiser's actions alienated many of the European nations, they also created alliances, directly between Germany and Austria-Hungary. As a consequence of the threat represented by these alliances, others were created between France and Russia, and between Britain and Belgium.

Britain was not being entirely altruistic in its alliance with small and defenceless Belgium. For centuries the Low Countries of Europe had been seen as the gateway to Britain, with only the might of the Royal Navy to prevent a seaborne invasion. Even in 1914 Britain would still be vulnerable if Belgium and her sea ports were held by a would-be invader.

After 1912 most governments in Europe felt that war with Germany was inevitable. With the assassination of Archduke Franz Ferdinand, heir to the Austro-Hungarian throne, and his wife, the Duchess Sophie, Germany found the excuse that it had been waiting for.

The assassination, by a Serbian anarchist, took place on 29 June 1914 in Bosnia. Bosnia had been annexed (a political word for what was actually occupation) by Austria-Hungary in 1908, and both the Serbs and Bosnians objected to the occupation.

Austria issued an ultimatum to Bosnia on 23 July 1914 demanding that the Serbian Army admit responsibility for the assassination, censor all anti-Austrian publications, remove all anti-Austrian agitators and suppress their organisations; Austria would also take part in the trials of the two Serbian army officers who were to take the blame for the assassination. Serbia was given just 48 hours to reply.

In the intervening period, Germany was busy canvassing the opinion of the heads of government of all the countries involved. If Austria invaded Serbia, would Russia help its fellow Slavs? If Russia intervened, would France then step in to help her Russian ally? If Russia and France became involved in the conflict, then how could Germany not help its ally, Austria? If Germany invaded Belgium to outflank the French Army, would Britain step in to defend Belgium? It was a merry-go-round that would end in tragedy.

The Serbian Government could never have agreed to Austria's outrageous demands, so on 25 July 1914 the Serbian Army was mobilised. From that moment events moved swiftly as the chain of alliances brought all of Europe into the conflict, culminating on 3rd August 1914 when Britain declared war on Germany after it had invaded France, Belgium, Luxembourg and Russian Poland.

In 1914 the British Expeditionary Force that went to the assistance of the French and Belgian armies consisted of six infantry divisions and a cavalry division, a total of 100,000 men. The Belgian Army numbered six infantry divisions and one cavalry division, a total of just over 100,000 men. The French Army numbered 62 infantry divisions and ten cavalry divisions, a total of 1,500,000 men. The German Army numbered 87 infantry divisions and 11 cavalry divisions, totalling just under two million men.

Britain's army was small, first, because since Oliver Cromwell's day Parliament has disliked large and expensive standing armies. Second, unlike most other European countries, Britain did not rely on conscription to man its army. More importantly, Britain's strength had always depended on the Royal Navy, the largest and best in the world. That it was able to blockade so many ports and virtually starve Germany into submission by 1918 is largely overlooked in histories of the First World War.

Therefore, judging purely on numbers committed, Britain would appear to have been the junior partner in the conflict, yet she would play a pivotal role throughout the First World War. If the British Army had not given its all on the Somme in 1916, Germany would not have had to divide its forces on the Western Front, and France would have buckled under the pressure at Verdun. If France had fallen, the war would have been over, with Germany the victor.

By the end of the war, Britain had mobilised 8,375,000, of which 702,410 were killed. France mobilised 8,500,000, losing 1,391,000. Germany mobilised 13,250,000, and 1,950,000 of them perished. In total there were 60 million combatants in the First World War, of whom 10 million were killed and 20 million irretrievably damaged in mind and body.

And to what end? With the benefit of hindsight, we know that the botched Versailles Treaty ensured that the First World War was only a dress rehearsal for the Second. Will we never learn a better way?

2
AUGUST 1914: FROM SHORNCLIFFE TO MONS

On 4 August 1914 at 6.40pm a telegram was received in the Officers Mess, Moore Barracks, at Shorncliffe near Folkestone. The Royal Irish Fusiliers were going to war. Although the Regimental Depot was still in Armagh, the 1st Battalion had been involved in basic exercises at different camps in England since 1908, and boredom had long since set in. For the subalterns the prospect of war heralded adventure and the chance of promotion.

After the mobilisation orders were read, the officers gathered in the anteroom of the Mess. The silence was broken by the question, 'Will company commanders wear spurs?' – such was the naivety and innocence of the junior officer class in the British Army. They little realised that they were soon to come up against the most formidable army in the world. They would soon find that in the trenches spurs would be of little use.

While the rest of the Battalion made preparation for a move to the Exhibition Hall in York, Captain Bull and Lieutenant Tuely were despatched to Armagh to place the Battalion Colours in the safe keeping of the Regimental Depot.

The Regimental Colours being taken back to Armagh for safe keeping for the duration of the war.

Let Sgt Wilson take up the story:

'BEING AN ACCOUNT OF THE TRIALS AND TEMPTATIONS OF A SERGEANT IN THE ROYAL IRISH FUSILIERS OF 10TH BRIGADE, 4TH DIVISION, BRITISH EXPEDITIONARY FORCE

FRANCE AND BELGIUM
25.08.14 TO 25.04.15

8 MONTHS ON THE SPREE

Stationed at Shorncliffe which is a very nice place, plenty of work to do as it contains many large training grounds. But for all the hard work which we go through in the shape of training, there are not many who would wish to change stations. Folkestone being about 1 mile away on one hand and the pretty historic village of Hythe on the other hand, it was always pleasant when the day's work was ended to visit either of these places.

During the winter months there were always plenty of amusements for the soldiers such as dances, whist drives etc. Shorncliffe being a garrison with 3 Regiments, 1 Brigade of Artillery and 1 Regt[1] of Cavalry and each in turn giving their monthly dance etc. It ran that every week one had one or other to go to. This is speaking from the Sgts[2] point of view when each mess entertains the other.

My stay however was to end soon, as the orders informed me I had been selected along with another Sgt of the Warwickshire Regt which was stationed by us, to proceed to Aberystwyth to instruct the Welsh Territorial Brigade in the use of the machine gun. I had qualified some time previously at Hythe in this subject and had come out well on my examination.

So on Friday the 24th July 1914 I set off along with my new comrade for Aberystwyth. As we did not arrive in London until 7.30pm we decided to remain in London for the night and leave first thing in the morning for our destination as we had not to commence our duties until the following Monday. We were lucky in obtaining nice beds in the Union Jack Club and after breakfast in the morning left for Euston. We caught our train which left at 11 am, and after a very tiresome journey arrived at Aberystwyth about 7 pm. As the camp was some few miles out and the last train had gone, there was nothing to do only find accommodation in town. We were successful in putting up with a nice old lady. The following day being Sunday we found that the first train to our camp did not leave until 1.30 pm, so we had the morning in looking round the fine prom and cliffs and spent a very pleasant time. At 1 pm we took ourselves to the Devils Bridge L Railway[3] and eventually arrived at our destination.

When we arrived we found the camp full and we got a tent to ourselves. The camp was in a lovely glen and for the next few days we had a nice time doing our drill amidst such nice surroundings. In the evenings we would go for walks and occasionally having a trip into Aberystwyth. The roads round this part of the country are lovely and many a stroll did we enjoy together, sometimes along the road we would meet schoolchildren and on being asked to sing, they would just band themselves together and give us some lovely songs in Welsh and we fairly enjoyed them.

We went on with our work until Monday the 3rd of August when we woke up in the morning and found that we were left almost alone, the whole camp having departed to some destination unknown to us. We two of the Regulars seemed to belong to no one and on asking should we stay or go back no one knew, and having no warrants for our return we seemed to be in a fix. However, we decided

1 Regiment

2 Sergeants

3 Devil's Bridge Light Railway, now preserved as the Vale of Rheidol Railway

between ourselves that if war had been declared it was our duty to go back, tickets or not, but before going we reported to the Brigade Major who gave us warrants for our return.

It was a very hot day I remember and we had some difficulty in getting our bits of baggage carried as all the wagons were in use or already gone. We managed however to have them put on a passing cart and ourselves also for which we were very glad. When we arrived at Aberystwyth we found all the town astir, what with it being Bank Holiday and crowded with visitors and also the scare of war and trains being stopped etc. It was quite lively, people rushing about trying to get trains back to their homes and others not knowing whether to go or stay on.

We eventually after some struggling found ourselves on the right train and after a long journey arrived back again in Shorncliffe at 2 am on Tuesday morning. Such an hour to arrive, every one in bed and knocking up storemen for blankets etc, it was some time before I got down to rest. On rising the next morning it seemed very quiet and no wonder for everyone had gone almost, only a few details being left in barracks. I found that the Battalion had got short move to the Isle of Sheppey in the Thames.'

Private P. Brady from Belturbet, Co Monaghan, was placed on the Army Reserve after serving with the Royal Irish Fusiliers during the Boer War. He was called up on the outbreak of war and was probably one of the 300 Reservists collected by Sgt Hugh Wilson from Armagh in late August 1914. Pte Brady was wounded in the back and arm during the fighting at Armentières on 20 October 1914. After recuperating at hospitals in Boulogne and Rouen he went back to the fighting and was wounded for a second time at St Julien on 25 April 1915. This photograph was taken during his convalescence at Erdington.

In 1908 there had been a fundamental reorganisation of the Army reserves. The Militia regiments were disbanded and replaced by the Territorial Force and the Special Reserve. From 1908, when a soldier joined up for a specific number of years he would spend part of it in the Regular Army, or with 'the Colours', and part of it on the Reserve. While on the Reserve he lived the life of a civilian, knowing that he would be immediately recalled for service if needed, especially in time of war.

At the outbreak of the Great War these Reservists[4] received their telegrams ordering them to report to their barracks. The *Armagh Guardian* reported that at 11pm on 8 August around 300 Reservists marched through the crowded streets of Armagh to the railway station. They were led by the band of the 3rd Battalion Royal Irish Fusiliers and the mounted troop of the Ulster Volunteers, followed by the local UVF Company, who were singing patriotic songs.

[4] No 9634 Pte Frank Alderman was one such Reservist, recalled to fight in the Great War. A native of Winchester, he joined the 1st Battalion Royal Irish Fusiliers when it moved to Aldershot in July 1908. After serving for the four years with 'the Colours' that he had signed up for, Pte Alderman left the Faughs, with a commitment to remain on the Reserve for a further eight years. He was killed in action at Armentières on 12 April 1915; his grave is unknown and he is commemorated on the Ploegsteert Memorial.

A number of the Nationalist Volunteers with St Malachy's band (who had been refused permission to march with the parade to the station) were waiting at the station and played and cheered as the soldiers marched through. Once inside the station the UVF formed into two lines as the soldiers marched past amid hearty cheers and wishes for a safe return, while the band of the 3rd Battalion played 'Auld Lang Syne'. The stationmaster, Mr McAllister, and his men sounded the fog signals as the train steamed on its way to Greenore. This was the first of four parties of men to leave Armagh to join the 1st Battalion.

The journal continues:

> 'It was very miserable for the next few days, with all being away, until I got orders to proceed to our Depot at Armagh to bring back reservists. I left on Friday and arrived at Armagh the following morning and had hardly time to look round and visit a few old friends before I was back again with 300 men for Shorncliffe. I had been previously stationed at Armagh for 3 years, so it was not strange to me. I left Armagh on Saturday night and oh such a send off we got, the streets were crowded and all along the line were fog signals which made an awful row as the train began to move. We had a nice quiet crossing, going by Greenore and Holyhead and arrived at Shorncliffe on Sunday.
>
> The following day I was placed as Sgt of the guard and sent to Folkestone to await the arrival of trains from London with Germans making to leave the country. I don't think any of them ever expected, but just to walk on board ship, so you can imagine their faces when they saw us lined up with fixed bayonets awaiting their arrival. We conducted them up to our gymnasium where they were searched and kept until such times as they could be removed to some permanent place, and so they kept arriving for no news having got to London, they knew nothing of the fate of their comrades who had left before.
>
> On the following day, Tuesday, I got the job of escort with a batch of them to Horsham where we handed them over for their permanent quarters. It was a very large building, belonging to the "blue coat boys"[5] and the only thing that was amiss was the beds, which being for boys were too small, but quite good enough for them I thought. On returning we were delayed and had to put up at the Union Jack Club as best we could, for the beds being all taken we slept in the reading room. The following day we managed after a lot of changing to finally arrive back at Shorncliffe and there were none of us sorry, I can safely say.

Royal Irish Fusiliers escort a party of Germans who had tried to board a ship at Dover to return to fight in their own country.

[5] The Blue Coat was the uniform worn by boys who went to Charity Schools in Britain.

Thursday the 13th I was warned for guard at the Folkestone Viaduct and remained on that Guard until Friday night when we were relieved. We would probably have been relieved before only the shortage of men at barracks make it impossible, the reserves having been sent on previously to the Battalion, a few only remaining.

During this time at Shorncliffe I was upset, thinking that the battalion would be ordered to the front and I not with them, so that I was constantly asking to be sent, urging that they had only one qualified machine gun sergeant with the battalion and the war footing was two. I got a telegram sent to the Adjutant and when, as I afterwards heard the Adjutant mention it to the CO, he said send for him at once saying he thought I was with the battalion the whole time. I was quite pleased when I got word I was to go, for the musketry instructor would have wished to have kept me with him.

On Sunday the 15th I left Shorncliffe with a party of 50 reserves for the battalion with an officer in charge. The battalion was now in York so we had a good long spin before us. Anyhow it passed off very nicely and we arrived late in the evening to find the battalion lying in the offices of the Rowntrees Chocolate works. A very large place, but uncomfortable for lying on as the floors were all concrete. We took up our time with mobilizing and I was lucky not to be in charge of a platoon. We did marches and got out occasionally in charge of an officer or NCO. We were allowed to go in the baths and everyone availed themselves of this. I remember a Sgt Scrafield cut his head open by diving too steep but not too bad as he was himself in a couple of days.'

The Faughs were now part of the 10th Brigade of the 4th Division, and together with the Seaforth Highlanders they moved to Darlington on 9 August, and were billeted in the local Drill Hall. This was part of a move to assemble the entire 4th Division on the East Coast as a precaution against invasion.

It was not until 18 August that the 10th Brigade was fully mobilised and could join the rest of the 4th Division at its tented encampment in Harrow Weald. Four days later, in the early hours of the morning, the Battalion marched to Kenton station

The boy soldiers of the Royal Irish Fusiliers at Shorncliffe before going off to war.

The railway station at Le Cateau where the Faughs detrained on 24 August 1914, ready to march into battle the next day.

to board two trains for Southampton Docks. When they disembarked from the SS *Lake Michigan* at Boulogne they marched through the town to cheers from the local inhabitants. It is remarkable that the French still turned out to encourage the soldiers even though they had been arriving in their thousands every day for over a week and a half.

After a march of one and a half miles they reached St Martin's Camp. Close by Napoleon gazed down at them from the top of the 'Colonne de la Grand Armeé', a monument erected on the spot where Napoleon had assembled his army prior to his intended invasion of England.

The Battalion began its move towards the enemy on 24 August, travelling by train via Amiens and St Quentin to Le Cateau, arriving in the afternoon. It was a short march to the bivouac at Inchy, and as the men moved south they passed large numbers of civilians engaged in digging long straight lines of trenches south of the Le Cateau-Cambrai road (this was most probably the locally recruited Civilian Guard, whose only uniform was an armband). This was the first time the local inhabitants had seen British soldiers, and 'souvenir hunters' caused much annoyance in and around the camp.

That evening the Battalion supply wagon arrived with rations and various supplies, including the first maps of France for the officers. At 2am the following morning the entire 10th Brigade marched from its bivouacs at Inchy, heading north towards St Python. The 4th Division, including the Royal Irish Fusiliers, was given the hazardous job of covering the retreat of the 3rd and 5th Divisions from Mons. Sgt Wilson describes the events:

> 'On Monday we got word that we were to move to Harrow on the morrow and so on Wednesday we were established at Harrow and remained there doing drill, marching etc and getting ourselves together, as with the reserves coming in it brought us well over strength and many of the men would be strangers to each other. We soon found ourselves out and got on well together, and we found that the whole division was formed up there, ready for moving at any moment, and we were all anxious to be off, so that when Friday came and we got our marching orders were all delighted for to be given a chance.
>
> At 12 noon we left our camp and entrained to arrive at Southampton on Saturday morning and embark. We sailed off at 10.30

am and were all day and night on board. We went that slow, always on the watch so that it was the afternoon of the following day before we sailed into Boulogne. We had a very nice passage over, but with that many being on board we could hardly find room to lie down, so that I kept on deck, but the rain came on during the night and we were a little uncomfortable. When we disembarked at Boulogne, we got our first sight of French soldiers who were on guard at the quay. They were quite delighted to see us and to see the antics of them trying to explain the difference in uniforms and weapons was comical. They were all death to the Germans and would go through the process of stabbing, shooting and cutting the throats of imaginary Germans.

When we had a little to eat and had everything off board we fell in and marched off all together with the other regiments of the Brigade.[6] We got a grand reception by the people, the whole cry being "Vive l' Angleterre", we answering "Vive le France". The people seemed greatly amused by the kilts of the Seaforths who were in our Brigade.

Marching up a steep hill we got into camp already put up with tents, which place we were told was where Napoleon had his army assembled for his invasion of England over a hundred years before. It was a vast place, but we were not to remain long there for no sooner had we had our supper than we were ordered to fall in and we stood to for some time until it was dark and then moved off to the station. We had a few camp fires burning but had to put them out when it got dark.

When we started off it was pitch dark and marching in close formation in the dark is not very pleasant, as one is liable to keep bumping into the one in front, and just as we started off a pack mule broke loose and caused some uneasiness. Our Regiment has cause to curse pack mules as in the Boer War, during a night attack the mules broke loose and nearly upset the whole column and also nearly resulted in disaster for our force.[7] This incident occurring when within close contact with the enemy. To carry on however, we arrived at the station and entrained about 12.30 and left soon afterwards for a destination unknown.

We got a little sleep in the carriage, as ours was not overcrowded, there only being four Sergeants in it. It would be early the following evening when we arrived at our final halting place having had a long ride and stopping occasionally for meals. We had some fun at one of the halts, for all hands turned out when the railway pump, a great big one, and I remember a very tall Sergeant of ours was under washing when one of the Sgts pulled the chain and he got a complete wash. He didn't fancy it at the first, but came round later. I think I was the cause of it, for from the carriage window I motioned one of the boys to pull the chain.

To proceed, we detrained at Le Cateau and from there marched about 12 miles. This was in the evening so it was rather pleasant than otherwise, that is to one that was trained, and I was and the majority of the Battalion, although this and longer marches later on, somewhat tired the reservists who had joined up from civilian life on mobilization and were now a little soft. After this march it being now night, we halted for about 4 hours and then again resumed our march, marching until day break, when we took up a position, digging ourselves in small trenches by the tools we carried with us.

Just before this order came, we were on the point of having our breakfast, the cooks having made a fire in a field just off the road

[6] See the Order of Battle in Appendix 4 for the Corps, Division and Brigade.

[7] On 30 October 1899 a detachment of Faughs were part of a night-time sortie before the siege closed around Ladysmith. As they walked into an ambush, the mules, which were carrying ammunition and the Maxim machine guns, stampeded and were lost. Without machine guns or a reserve of ammunition the soldiers were exposed to the withering Boer rifle fire. As well as numerous casualties, the Boers took 493 prisoners.

Above Sgt Wilson commented on the leafy fields of mangols, or sugar beet, in which he sought shelter when under shell fire for the first time on 26 August 1914. The sugar beet is harvested in the autumn, and heaps of sugar beet destined for the *sucerie* or sugar factory are still a common site in northern France.

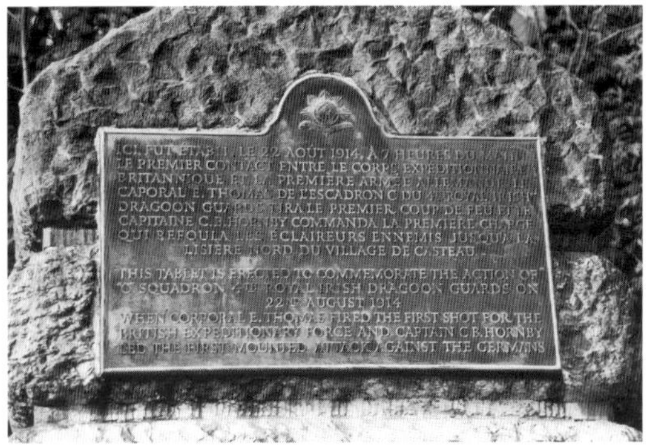

Top This plaque near Mons commemorates the first British shot fired in the Great War by the 4th Royal Irish Dragoons on 22 August 1914.

Above Almost directly opposite the above plaque is another marking the last British shot fired in the Great War, which was in almost exactly the same spot on 11 November 1918.

and had the tea made and were just giving it out when the order came to extend and intrench, so we had to do without our breakfast and a good many times in the near future also did we miss. Well we were no sooner in our little holes, and lying quite comfortable looking at the beauty of the mangol[8] by which we were surrounded when we experienced the feeling of being first under shell fire. For they must have observed our position, as no doubt they did from their aeroplane which was flying over us.'

The 10th Brigade took position in trenches around Fontaine-au-Tertre Farm. Major Phibbs's Company had to dig in to the south-west of Quievy. Random firing could be heard throughout the afternoon, mostly from cavalry patrols and lorry-mounted machine guns. These units were employed on reconnaissance but inevitably ended up skirmishing with the enemy. The Faughs, who were on the extreme left of the Brigade, experienced their first contact with the enemy. They now realised that they were up against superior and better-equipped soldiers.

As darkness fell, confusion reigned and orders were received to withdraw to a new position in and around the village of Haucourt. The 10th Brigade

[8] Sugar beet

was to act as rearguard, with the Faughs on the flank. The route took the 1st Battalion via Herpigny Farm, west of Bethencourt and Beauvois, and the roads were in such bad condition that the Battalion's bicycles had to be abandoned. The only illumination in the pitch-dark night came from burning farms and haystacks to the north.

At approximately 6am on 26 August the Faughs and Seaforth Highlanders reached the cemetery at Haucourt. At this point the 10th Brigade had been detailed as Divisional Reserve, and the weary and footsore soldiers were able to fall out and rest; soon the vast majority of the men were fast asleep on the ground with no shelter other than their greatcoats. Unfortunately, it was to be a short rest, as Sgt Wilson describes:

> 'There was a town in front of us which we took for Mons and parts of it were on fire and from this direction it was that the German gunners were firing on us. Anyhow, as we were beginning to get accustomed to them going over our heads and chaffing each other we got the order to retire. We did not much relish this as we were in expectation of having a closer acquaintance with their infantry, and again we knew that as soon as we stood up we would get the shells all the more. Still it had to be done and we were very lucky for we retired from that field without loosing one.
>
> As soon as we got out of sight from the enemy we came across the French who were intrenched on our right and as we passed them they were firing for all they were worth at a German aeroplane which has hovering above us. We kept in good formation and retired for about one mile and we were the first back and so again we were extended and took up position again while the remaining troops passed us by, leaving us face to face again with the enemy. As it was now dark it was hard to distinguish friend from foe coming back and it was here lying along side my section by the railway that I saw the first ambulances pass by with the wounded. After some hours lying in the position waiting for the moment when we would first catch sight of the enemy, we again were moved off. It was now raining and we did not feel in the best of spirits with this retiring, having never been in the habit of thinking of it and not having fought much up to the present we could not understand it. We were carrying our full marching order[9] and at this time of the year, being so hot during the day, it was pretty hard work.'

In the early hours of 26 August heavy machine gun fire was heard from the north: the cavalry and lorry-mounted Jäger battalions of the German II Corps were assaulting the outposts of the 4th Division. The Faughs immediately moved south of Haucourt and deployed 'A' Company to the east of the village, 'D' Company to the west of the village, 'C' Company to the left of 'D', and 'B' Company in support.

As the initial skirmishing died away the German infantry of III and IV Corps did not engage the British troops but rather let the artillery duel between both sides commence at about 8am. With the British guns both out-ranged and outnumbered, casualties began to mount and guns had to be destroyed as a tactical withdrawal turned into full retreat. The journal continues:

> 'The next morning, the 26th, found us formed up to give battle. We were all in close formation lying behind a rise of ground, so we could not be seen by the enemy. The ground was wet after the recent rain, and as we wanted to rest as much as possible, we all got a sheaf of corn to lie on. Then we would get

[9] In 1914 a British Army infantry soldier in full marching order carried his rifle and wore either a leather or canvas webbing belt, which had shoulder braces attached with brass fittings. The following would normally be attached: ammunition pouches with 150 rounds of .303 ammunition; haversack with greatcoat, spare clothing and especially clean, dry socks; knapsack with washing and shaving equipment, waterproof ground sheet (which doubled as a cape when it rained), emergency rations, wound dressings and sand bags; bayonet and scabbard; entrenching tool and pouch; water bottle; and additional ammunition bandoliers.

moved again and perhaps just a few yards one way or the other, so that we had to drop our bundles of straw, but when we would halt again, there would be a proper scramble to run back to get our beds again so that in the end, when we moved, not knowing how far we would go, we carried them with us.

Our artillery then began firing on our left and it was not so long before they began to get shelled back. We were only resting a few yards away from them and we were enjoying the struggle first rate, but soon began to realise it was not play, for first one and then the other gun would get smashed up and the gunners were falling also. So that in the finish there was only one gun remaining and it was splendid the way the gunners worked it and in the end got it away with only half the horses and men. We now noticed our cavalry returning over the crest in front of us and poor fellows they fairly got it. We could see horses and men falling and one man I saw went back to bring his wounded comrade with him, when he got knocked over too.

It must be remembered that their force in guns and men were over treble to what we had as we afterwards learned, so that it was best to retire and so save as many as possible. We would not have retired had we our way, but orders had to be obeyed. At least our turn came to advance and we went forward by sections. My company was on the extreme left and my section the last to go, so that I expected we would get it hot going over the crest in front, for that was where they got our cavalry and they had the range exactly.

However as the other platoons passed over safely in front of me, I thought we would escape. I remember as we were going up we met a young officer of some other Regiment coming back wounded, his face was bleeding, also his arm. He said as he passed us, "Where are you going?" I said pointing in front, "Over there to attack." He said as he went on "God help you". I thought he might have kept his prayers for some better occasion, but no doubt he was excited with being wounded, or would not have said it as it would have been likely to discourage us.'

The 1st Battalion war diary records that the most memorable feature of 26 August was the lull that descended on the battlefield in the early afternoon. Remembered as lasting from one to two hours, it was a strange sultry silence in the August sunshine. It was said that even the birds did not sing, overawed by the recent thundering of the guns. It was at this point that several of the British regiments reported seeing angelic hosts sweeping from the heavens towards the Germans, driving them away from the British soldiers.

This is one of many reported sightings by British soldiers of angels and ghostly figures during the period of the retreat from Mons and the Battle of Le Cateau. Today these sightings, which were undoubtedly hallucinations caused by starvation and exhaustion, are referred to collectively as the 'Angel of Mons'[10]. Considering that up to this point the Germans had been winning the battle, it is inexplicable why their next move was to retreat from the battlefield, rather than press their advantage with an infantry advance.

To the Faughs it seemed that the enemy had had enough – German infantry was observed retiring from the northern ridges. In fact, the Germans were concentrating more guns, and by 4pm their artillery had commenced such a storm of steel that those who survived the four years of war compared it to the bombardments of 1918.

Later in the day Lieutenant Olphert's Platoon from 'B' Company was sent to reinforce 'A' Company. The Battalion also lent support to the Seaforths and Royal Dublin Fusiliers, also in the 10th Brigade. Apart from this, all other positions were maintained. Battalion Headquarters, together with, 'B', 'D' and part of 'C' Company, eventually bivouacked in the vicinity of Hurlevent Farm to the south-east of Selvigny.

Brigadier Haldane's communication problems were compounded by the lack of a Signal Company, and not all urgent messages to withdraw

[10] See Appendix 3

After marching all night, at 6am on 26 August 1914 the Faughs and the Seaforths reached Haucourt village. They sought shelter within the cemetery walls and immediately lay down and slept. In this communal cemetery the memorials to the right and left of the Cross of Sacrifice commemorate those soldiers of the Faughs and Seaforths who were killed at Haucourt and who are buried in this cemetery.

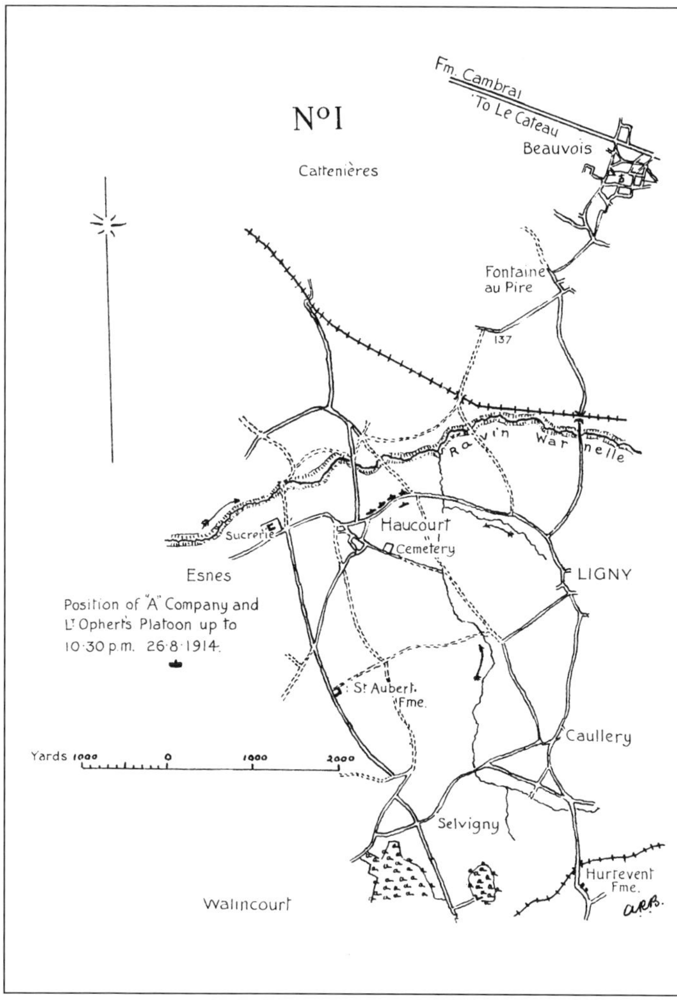

Map showing the area around Haucourt and the defensive positions established by the Faughs in the village.

The memorial to an unknown Sergeant of the Royal Irish Fusiliers buried in Haucourt Communal Cemetery. This can only be 10274 Sgt Charles Blair Godwin, who is known to have been killed by Lt Olphert's side when their platoon led a charge on the German lines at Haucourt village on 26 August 1914.

were received by such as 'A' Company (with Lieutenant Olphert's Platoon attached). They had previously been ordered by a staff officer to dig in along the Haucourt to Ligny Road and 'hold the position till all was blue'.

As the members of 'A' Company prepared to stay the night they heard German words of command and a bugle call from within Haucourt village. Immediately all platoon commanders formed their men to meet the attack. Lieutenant Olphert led his men in a charge against the enemy and was first shot in the foot, then the head. Sergeant Godwin, his second in command, was killed by his side.[11]

Sgt Wilson continues his account:

'To go on – the rest having passed over, our turn came and I being in command was just a couple of paces in rear of the section. All was going well and I had them well extended and strange to see we all still carried our sheaves, so that I am sure we could be seen for miles when, as we got to the crest, a shell burst as it seemed to me right on my head. I fell down and was just wondering what happened when I heard groans coming from all round me. The man in front of me was kicking nearly in my face and when I looked I could see he was in his death throes. I got his bandage out and when I went to start to bandage him I did not know where to begin, for he had that many holes in him. I counted seven, but there was in all probability more. Anyhow I put the bandage on the most serious one I thought, that was in the throat, but I might have spared myself the trouble for as I finished I noticed he had one through the heart. He died before I left him.

As I was doing this, others were calling me who had been wounded and as I looked round I saw that the whole section had been practically put out, there being only a L/Cpl and man besides myself left. I went on to the rest who was not as quite as serious, but the shells started bursting over our heads, so that it was not a comfortable job. One bullet coming past my head and just grazing the man I was putting the bandage on. I could have gone on to the rest only I thought the Captain would be wondering why I had not come on, so I decided to leave them for the time being and go on. I was sorry to do so as there was one poor chap wounded horribly, his chest lying open. It was

[11] Sgt Charles Blair Godwin from Willesden, Middlesex, was educated at Marlborough College, and was killed in action on 26 August 1914. This popular young soldier had shown great promise as a leader and would undoubtedly been commissioned as an officer, had he lived. He currently has no known grave and is commemorated at La Ferté-sous-Jouarre memorial. When I recently visited Haucourt Communal Cemetery I found a memorial marking the nearby grave of a Sergeant of the Royal Irish Fusiliers who was killed on 26 August 1914 at Haucourt. According to official casualty lists and the Regimental archives, Sgt Godwin was the only Royal Irish Fusiliers Sergeant killed on that date at Haucourt. I have contacted the Commonwealth War Graves Commission with a view to having this acknowledged as the final resting place of this fine soldier.

a warm corner that, for they still kept sending their shells and bursting them in dozens. I began to think I was not going to be hit for they were cutting the ground up all round me.

When I went on I found that the rest of the company was not so far on as I expected, but were just lying down firing about 200 yards on, close to the border of another mangol[12] field. I reported to the Captain and he asked where the rest of the section was and I told him that we had a bit of hard luck crossing the ridge and that they were all killed or wounded. Where I was then was not so bad for shell fire, but we were getting a good share of rifle fire. We could see the Germans running about on the rise in front of us, but the distance was a little too far for accurate rifle fire. Just then one of ours near me got one through the brain but it did not kill him outright, as they led him away raving. As I looked to the front again, a bullet just grazed the man next to me and he picked it up and put it in his pocket, saying it was quite warm. I said it would have been warmer if it had taken that old nose of yours off. He had a pretty decent nose too.

There was a road running down the hill in front of us and the Germans were coming down it in droves so our artillery I was glad to see spotted them from somewhere and by jove they did get it. They just bursted them lovely, one a little further up than other and every time the smoke went away we could see it had left them in heaps. While watching this I had forgotten about the wounded behind, so suddenly remembering I asked permission from the Captain to go and help to finish bandaging them and try and get them away, so he let me go. There was another man just then who had got a nasty wound in the leg, so I went back with him. We had some trouble to carry him, and I afterwards heard he had been taken prisoner.

When I got back to the wounded I found them lying there still, but I had thought that they might have been moved by the stretcher bearers. While going to them I came under some heavy fire but when I got where they were I did the best I could for them. The man who was wounded in the chest was dying I could see, so we carried him back a little and also the dead men. We laid him beside them, but we should have thought better, for he asked us who they were as we had their faces covered up and we said some men who had been badly shook and wanted to lie quiet and for him not to try to talk to them. Poor chap. I often wonder what the Germans did with him for we had to leave him.

I and the L/Cpl who came with me then went back and oh it was hot, simply raining shells, the men were coming back in dozens wounded and the blood running off them. We tried to get another way round and so back to the company, but we seemed to get into a warmer place than ever, and had to lie down by the side of the road while a perfect hurricane of shells passed over. When we got to the company, they were digging trenches for themselves as hard as they could go amidst a proper bombardment.

When we had finished and lay down in what little hole we had time to dig, we began to get ready for them, for by this time they were very near. We would see our shells bursting just over the crest in front and we afterwards learned that they did fearful havoc with the Germans who were massed there in their usual formation. We had to keep very low and would have wished to have been able to get into the earth itself, for the shells were coming very low. One chap lifted his head to look round and a shell took it off completely. The escapes were marvellous, a Sergeant afterwards found a shrapnel bullet embedded in his bible, another his buttons shot off his jacket and several found when they went to get their mess tins from their packs that they were no use having been riddled with bullets. I found a German bullet in my pocket and never could remember how it got there.

[12] Sugar beet

Hurriedly dug, shallow and cramped trenches were typical of the early weeks of the war; they did not provide much cover or comfort for the soldiers.

A Company of the King's Own Regiment got almost cut up to a man with machine gun fire, they were a little to our right and got caught while digging trenches. It was now about 3.30 and the order was passed along to retire, and this was taken up by platoons retiring individually. We did get it though for no sooner had we risen to go back than they poured shell and rifle fire into us, but through it all I did not see one man running. We simply went back at the same steady pace as we had advanced. After retiring some distance we got into a little rough ground and with men from other Companies being there we got moved up and so had to act more or less for ourselves. I got down with several others into a deep gully and they must have spotted us for no sooner were we in than you would have thought they were trying to blow us, ground and all up. The shells simply poured on us, they were firing battery fire 6 at a time. Some of the men were looking for an outlet from this death trap and we were by then pretty well messed up.

The Lce Cpl[13] who was with me before, during the time we were attending to the wounded, was by my side and he said, "You seem pretty lucky, I am going to stick by you until the finish." I said, "You stick by me, I will get you out if I can." So I went or rather crawled a little farther up and found a way across the open. It seemed the only way out so I said, "We had better get out, run and chance it." So the two of us got up and away. We had to drop several times for want of breath, but luckily were not easily seen as the corn here was standing and consequently high. It was touch and go though for the bullets were whistling all round us. Another few sprints and we managed to come down on to a road out of view. Here we found all arms winding their way to the rear, so trudged along with them. After marching along for about half a mile we came to a cross roads and there we were pleased to see an officer of our Regiment forming up the men as they came along. We accordingly fell in and when we numbered about 100, the majority being our own Company, a Staff Officer rode up and told us off for a new position.'

The attack was broken and the Germans fled. 'A' Company now found itself cut off from its Brigade and the main force, and although the men had fought off the last German attack, they were now almost totally surrounded. Unsure as to the whereabouts of the rest of the Battalion, the Company's senior officers held a conference at

[13] Lance Corporal

midnight. The decision was made to proceed to the rendezvous point at the crossroads to the north-east of the village, which was reached after marching for a couple of hours. There they met up with other stragglers from the Warwickshire Regiment under the command of a Major Poole. Poole's little column followed the same route as the main body of the Faughs, but never caught up with them until they reached Le Câtelet.

Under Poole's command the men made their way south through Selvigny. With great skill and daring he led the small column back towards its own lines, often within actual sight of the enemy. Major Gray became ill on the march and had to be carried, first on horseback and later in a small cart. He eventually had to be left in the care of a Red Cross dressing station. The journal continues:

> 'We had thought now that it was getting on towards evening, we would have got a bit of a rest, but no, we were marched along and advanced across the fields and told to lie down by platoons. I was in the 3rd platoon then, and we were lying one behind the other. The order came then to advance to attack and the first platoon extended and moved down out of sight over the crest line. After a short while they came back, that is what was left of them. One of the enemy's aeroplanes just now came into view flying very low and of course soon spotted us. It then began to drop coloured lights which were a signal to their artillery where we were, and then again I began to wonder would we come out of this day alive. Luckily for us the shells went the least thing too far or else we were doomed. The Staff Officer made his appearance again and gave orders to advance again. The platoon in front then went forward, but could make no headway as the fire was that deadly.
>
> I was just waiting my turn when the order came again to get out of it as quick as possible. So we marched out on to the road again and I remember just as we were going a shell burst over us, but luckily did little damage, a man by me had one of his fingers blown off by a piece. We went through a little village, the name I think was Ligny and oh it was a mess. The houses were all smashed up and some of them on fire, overturned guns, wagons, lying in the road and mixed up with them all were dead horses and men. There was a small place I saw was rigged up as a hospital and the wounded who were in were all captured, as there was no time to take them with us. We started on our march through the night and so for nights afterwards we kept going as we afterwards found.
>
> This had been a very bad day for us, but considering the numbers who were opposing us we did very well indeed, and also taking into consideration the amounts of shell fire we underwent, the casualties were slight. As we afterwards found out the numbers against us were nearly 10 times our own, so it was surprising we were not all killed or captured. I think our bold front had a lot to do with it, for we advanced to them as if we were on parade and one Sgt with his platoon went on too far and so little did he think of the numbers against him, that he must have charged into a whole Brigade. Anyhow nothing has ever been heard of him or his platoon since. The men were so indifferent, that you would smile to see them in the midst of all the fire during their retreat across the open, deliberately stop and undo the pack of some dead man and take out his rations, and then go calmly on.'

By this point the men were starving, their rations had long since run out, and no new supplies could reach them during this chaotic retreat. They resorted to a diet of apples from local orchards. Despite their own hunger and exhaustion they did what they could for the numerous refugees that crowded the roads.

Major Poole led his command over the bridge across the River Somme at Ham, just before the engineers destroyed it. Here they met up with the British rearguard and the men were very glad to make the next stage of the journey to Compiègne in wagons and lorries. During this part of the journey Lieutenant O'Donovan and his No 4 Platoon somehow became separated. They had an adventurous few days and went as far south as Le

During the chaos of the retreat from Mons many soldiers became separated from their main unit. Lance Sergeant Ball, who was with Lt O'Donovan's Platoon, went as far south as Le Mans before they managed to find the Faughs again. Lance Sergeant Ball died of wounds received during the retreat in the hospital at Le Mans and was buried nearby.

The grave of Lt Roger Owen Birbeck Wakefield in Caudry Old Communal Cemetery. He was wounded during the defence of Caudry village on 28 August 1914. Despite being carried to safety by Sgt Stevenson, he succumbed to his wounds later that day.

Mans, before they managed to find the Battalion again on 7 September.

At the village of Caudry the 4th Division transport was attacked. During the action that followed Lieutenant Roger Wakefield, the Faughs' Transport Officer, was wounded. Under heavy fire his Sergeant dashed out and dragged him to safety, but when Sgt Stevenson realised that the wound was mortal he had to leave his officer and return to the lines. Lt Wakefield died the next day from his wounds and was buried at Caudry Old Communal Cemetery. After the action the Battalion transport marched south through St Quentin, commanded by Lieutenant T. E. Bunting DCM.

Sgt Wilson continues his journal:

'We marched from this on until daybreak, then with a short rest on again through the whole day, with the constant sound of the shells bursting in our rear. We marched on and on until nearly evening when we halted for a short spell. Then, on again, all through Friday night, marching until daybreak, we did 20 miles that night. And such marching, going on for a few minutes then a check, when we would just lie or drop down on the road, then kicked up and on again. A short rest and move on with frequent rests throughout the day. Sometimes we would at one of these halts, try and make some tea, but no sooner had the water began to boil than the order came "Fall in" and we would then have to throw it out, so that we really did not know how long we would remain halted, or if we would have time to make a meal. Speaking of meals – what we had at this time was very scanty and we relied mostly on the inhabitants for what we got. The French were very good giving us what they had. We would have given a lot to get a cigarette this time, as I don't think there was a packet in the whole Battalion.'

At dawn on 27 August the troops of the 4th and 5th Divisions converged on the village of Le Câtelet. The men had marched all night in torrential rain, and as the day grew hot and humid their sodden serge uniforms became extremely uncomfortable. The 4th Division was sent to the Vendhuille Road, where the men made contact with the main column and had their first meal for many days. As they ate they watched the French military engineers destroy the railway line just south of the village of Roisel.

The 4th Division was concentrated in the area of Haucourt, the 10th Brigade again acting as rearguard in the area of Nobescourt Farm. Expecting an imminent German attack, the Faughs and Seaforths prepared defensive positions: farm buildings were barricaded, loopholes dug in walls and trenches excavated. Exhausted after all the marching and counter-marching of the last few weeks, many of the men collapsed. The expected German attack did not materialise, and as darkness fell the march was resumed. Iron-shod boots on the French paved roads rang out through the night as the Battalion passed through the villages of Tertry, Monchy, Lagache, Croix and Matigny. At dawn the Somme was crossed and the entire Battalion was reunited at Voyennes.

At first light on 28 August the Faughs were on the move again as the 10th Brigade took up a position to the south of Canizy and parallel to the Somme Canal, to cover the withdrawal of the 3rd Division. Acting as rearguard (again!) they proceeded via Esmery, Hallon, Flavy-le-Moldeux, Tirlancourt and Muirancourt to Bussy, eventually reaching the latter about midnight.

That evening, when the muster roll was called, 136 officers and men were found to be missing, lost during the chaotic retreat. Many soldiers from other British regiments ended up in the same fix. Two of the lost soldiers from the Faughs were Privates Thomas Donohoe and David Martin, who had taken refuge in a ditch near the village of Villeret. They had been joined by another soldier, Pte William Thorpe of the King's Own Lancaster Regiment. Hiding out in a nearby wood, they came upon a fourth lost soldier, Pte Robert Digby of the Hampshires. After a few days of a hand-to-mouth existence, scavenging in the woods, Digby persuaded the villagers of Villeret to take them into hiding.

This was a dangerous undertaking, as Villeret was now in German-occupied France, and by the end of September two German regiments would be billeted in and around the village. The soldiers were utterly trapped. They hid out in haylofts, attics or wardrobes, and, as the months wore on, the four soldiers abandoned their uniforms, and in an attempt to try and blend in they began to wear civilian clothes.

Thomas Donohoe came from Killybandrick in Co Cavan, and was aged 32. When the war started he had been married to Bridie for four years. David Martin had been brought up in the Castlereagh area of Belfast and was aged 28. He was also married, and had worked as a cook before joining the Army.

The four soldiers remained hidden in Villeret, behind German lines, for almost two years. Speaking fluent French, Robert Digby had more freedom than the other three. He became very friendly with the family who were sheltering him and fell in love with their daughter, and fathered a child, Hélène.

Many British soldiers were in hiding behind the German lines. Searching for these potential spies was time-consuming and the Commander in Chief of the German Army decided to issue an amnesty: all enemy soldiers hiding out in German-occupied France were to give themselves up by 30 April 1916. Posters were put up in all villages close to the lines stating that all those who surrendered before the deadline would be treated as prisoners of war – all those arrested after the deadline would be shot.

Panic gripped Villeret. The four soldiers tried to escape from the village, but found it impossible to cross the German lines. They did not trust the Germans enough to surrender to them, and feared that, amnesty or not, they would be shot as spies. They returned to Villeret on 25 April and went into hiding again.

When the German military police entered Villeret on 16 May 1916 they knew exactly where to search – there is no doubt that one of the villagers had given the soldiers away. Thorpe, Donohoe and Martin were caught quickly, but Digby managed to escape to the local woods. Reprisals on the villagers began immediately: the Mayor, the postman and their families were arrested and taken away with the soldiers to nearby Le Câtelet. The villagers received either hefty fines or between eight and ten years imprisonment with hard labour. The soldiers were not so lucky. To prevent further reprisals on the villagers, and especially his family, Robert Digby gave himself up five days later.

The four soldiers had a trial of sorts; all were accused of spying, and all were sentenced to death by firing squad. On their last evening, one of the villagers retrieved their uniforms from their hiding place and brought them to Le Câtelet prison. Thorpe, Donohoe and Martin walked proudly in uniform through the village just before dawn the next morning, 27 May 1916. Tied to posts beneath the ruined rampart walls of Le Câtelet castle, the firing squad of 12 German soldiers stepped forward. The three soldiers were buried in Le Câtelet's tiny graveyard beside the Escaut River.

The following day was Sunday, and when the priest arrived at the church he found the graves covered in flowers, and the church packed with people. Every flower was a mark of respect, and a gesture of defiance and support for Robert Digby, who was to be executed the next evening. Digby wrote his final letters, to his mother and family in England and also to his family in Villeret. His last wish was to be buried in Villeret, near his family.

The Mairie or Town Hall at Le Câtelet. With its barred basement windows, it is possibly the 'prison' where Privates Donohoe, Martin, Thorpe and Digby spent their last night on earth.

The memorial plaque that marks the spot on the rampart walls of Le Câtelet where Privates Donohoe, Martin, Thorpe and Digby were executed by the Germans. Unfortunately barbed wire fences prevent public access to the memorial.

Le Câtelet church: the soldiers' graves can be seen to the immediate left of the church through the gateway.

The graves of Privates Thorpe, Donohoe and Martin (*above*) and Private Digby (*right*) in Le Câtelet churchyard.

Not only was that denied him, but he was buried in the furthermost corner of Le Câtelet graveyard, apart from his comrades. In 1999 the people of Villeret and Le Câtelet dedicated a plaque on the spot were the bullet holes still show in the ruined rampart walls of Le Câtelet castle.

Returning to the actions of the Regiment, 29 August 1914 would see the Faughs at last get a brief rest and the opportunity to clean themselves and their weapons. The Battalion had its first view of aerial combat as an Allied plane chased an enemy machine back across the lines. At about 11pm, acting as rearguard, the Battalion moved to Beaurains and halted for some time during the cold dark night in what appeared to be the grounds of a chateau. The stillness was suddenly disrupted by a few men, yelling madly, bursting out of an outhouse. They turned out to be French civilians who had mistaken the Faughs' Irish accents for Prussians.

Sgt Wilson takes up the story:

> 'We were resting for a few hours when the order came again to move, this was Saturday night the 29th. We marched on through this night and at dawn on the following morning, found us going through the town of Noyan[14]. Here we passed through and over the river and then halted. My platoon got the order to go back again as the Ulans[15] were reported to be

[14] In Noyon, the building used as the present-day town's Hospitalier was, in 1914, the HQ of the 9th Regiment of Cuirassiers (French cavalry).

[15] German cavalry; the proper spelling is Uhlans.

The perimeter wall and gate into the grounds of the ruined chateau at Beaurains. The Faughs slept in the grounds on the night of 29 August 1914. The chateau had been destroyed during the Franco-Prussian war of 1870-71.

entering the town and so were too close on our heels. Under our officer we went back into the town again and he split us up in the centre of the town, my section being sent up a street on the left leading out on to the open country. The town was apparently deserted, not a soul to be seen, but when we got to the end of the street, an old man came out and gave us some bread and wine and we were very thankful for it, as we were very hungry, having had nothing for many hours. From our position we could see several moving about and had pot shots at

These plaques on the hospital wall at Noyon commemorate the dead of the 9th Regiment of Cuirassiers. During the early days of the war this French cavalry regiment suffered heavy casualties, perhaps partly due to their still wearing the colourful but impractical uniform of Napoleon's army of 1815.

them. Some of our cyclists came in afterwards with several prisoners and trophies they had taken, such as Ulans lances, horses and helmets.

As we would have to move out of the town at a smart pace when the order came, I sent the men with sore feet on now and it was well I did for otherwise they would have been left, for we caught them up just as we crossed the bridge, and we were no sooner over than our engineers blew it up. They blew all the bridges up along this part, and it seemed a pity to see such lovely bridges destroyed. Anyhow, it was to delay the enemy and so for our safety.

From here we marched on again with very little rest. This part of the retirement was about the worst, as the days were so hot and not having time to get a proper meal it began to tell on the men. Poor fellows they did their best, but could not help from falling out, and then if we got a short halt, they would come limping in again. A good many during the heat of the day would fall down in fits by the side of the road. We lost a good many like this, and I often wondered what became of them. Taken prisoners or should have been, but we had heard later of the Ulans killing all that they came across, and when previously we had crossed the river some noticed one of our men who had been unable to cross with us, taken by the Ulans into a farm yard. They however came out without him.

One of our men who got left, but afterwards joined us, said he outdone the Ulans lovely. They came across him lying down in a wood, and thought he was wounded, and so he pretended to be. They then went back to bring a stretcher for him, but as soon as he got them away, he climbed up a tree, and when they came back, he said it was great to see the rage they were in. He dodged them and later managed to join us again.'

The Faughs made it across the bridges at Pont l'Evèque just minutes before it was blown up in an attempt to slow or halt the German advance on 30 August 1914.

At 6.45am on 30 August the 1st Battalion arrived at the bridge over the Oise at Pont l'Evèque. They had to hold the bridge while the Sappers prepared it for demolition and until Major Phibbs and 'D' Company caught up with the rest of the Battalion. During the retreat 'D' Company had been almost cut off and it was only thanks to the 4th Division Cyclist Company skirmishing with a party of Uhlans[16] that allowed 'D' Company to rejoin the rest of the Battalion.

The Battalion continued on its way, through Carlepont, Tracey-le-Mont, Berneuil-sur-Aisne to Genancourt, which was reached at 10pm. Here a bivouac was established in a field to the south of the town and a welcome supper was provided from the supply wagons.

On the last day of August the 4th Division moved through the Forest de Compiègne in two columns; the 10th Brigade marched with the right, or the most northern column, and so was nearest the enemy. A sharp lookout had to be kept, as Uhlans were reported to be patrolling the forest. At some point during the day's march the Faughs were ordered to form a rearguard for the left of the column. After dark they reached St Sauveur, so exhausted that they simply bivouacked in the streets of the town. Here the troops heard that the French Fifth Army under General Lanrezac had driven the Germans back at Guise.

The journal describes events:

'We kept marching off and on throughout the day until evening when we came into a village called Cuise la Motte in the province of Oise. As we were passing through this village we got word that we were going to rest for the night outside, and indeed we wanted it, for we thought we were never going to stop. As we

On 30 August 1914 the entire 4th Division moved through the Forest de Compiègne in two columns, ever watchful for patrolling German cavalry.

16 German cavalry

passed through the village the inhabitants came out and ran into the ranks giving us drink and bits of bread. This was very good of them, but used to cause a little confusion in the ranks, men stopping to drink and so staying others behind. Some got straying behind and I was told to bring them in, and after chasing them as best we could for I had met another Sergeant and the two of us kept together, for it was now dark.

It was a problem to know how far the Battalion had gone on, and I must confess that we transgressed this time. We were so weary and tired that we would have lain ourselves down anywhere and gone straight to sleep. Anyhow, the two of us set up a side street and fell in with a nice party who gave us plenty to eat and we had a good time. For now were starting to pick a few words of the language up and could get on very well together. As it got late, they said they could find us a place to sleep and so the old man and his wife took us out on to the main road again where he unlocked the door of a large house. It was a lovely house and when he shewed us our bed we were simply delighted. It was a chance going to bed with the Germans so near, but we didn't care and so got in. You can imagine how we felt in a bed after being so long undergoing outdoor sleeping accommodation. So we were not long in removing our heavy packs off us, for I still kept mine, although a large number had either thrown them away, not been able to march with the weight or else had lost them.[17]

[17] As already described in note 9, in 1914 a British Army infantry soldier wore either a leather or canvas webbing belt, which had shoulder braces attached with brass fittings. The following would normally be attached: ammunition pouches with 150 rounds of .303 ammunition; haversack with greatcoat, spare clothing and especially clean, dry socks; knapsack with washing and shaving equipment, waterproof ground sheet (which doubled as a cape when it rained), emergency rations, wound dressings and sand bags; bayonet and scabbard; entrenching tool and pouch; water bottle; and additional ammunition bandoliers.

Left In the late evening of 31 August 1914, the 10th Brigade reached St Sauveur. The men were so exhausted that they simply fell asleep in the village streets and bivouacked on the square in front of the village church.

Right A French demarcation stone marking the limit of the German advance. It is located on the side of the D145 near Autreches. Rarely, it still has some of its original blue paint.

So we heard nothing more after the old man and his wife had left us, until morning when they woke us up with breakfast lying on the table. However we got nicely cleaned up before we thought of eating and just as we were about to start, the people we could see commenced to run out of their houses and put the shutters up in the windows and locking all doors. So we got word the Ulans were here again on top of us, and we had to move quickly but for all we did not like leaving our nice breakfast. I don't think we would have left it had they been at the door, so we made a sandwitch as best we could and ran out eating it along the street.

I think we two would be about the last of the British out of that place for we did not see a soul, and began to think we would either be captured and cornered and have to fight before we could come up with our Battalion. Anyhow, we were lucky for they must have been in one street as we went out of the other, but we kept on and after a while came up to our Rear Guards and soon then to the Battalion. We were nice and clean looking and the other chaps began chaffing us. I thought we would have got into a scrape for the Coy Major mentioned something about getting shot for being absent. I think it was worth the chance as we couldn't resist it.

We had not long joined them when they began to move off and we marched all through this day in the burning sun. Towards dusk we halted for a while and by this time a good number of the men were feeling very fatigued. So during this night as the movement had to be kept on they picked the worst of the men out and put them up on the artillery limbers[18], so that every gun and limber was packed. The gunners themselves walking to let the tired infantry men ride. I did not go with this party as I was feeling quite fit, only a little tired, but my feet were not troubling me. The men who were to walk were marched off then and one man who was riding took my pack off me to take on the wagon, but I never saw it again. I missed it too, for besides my great coat and mess tin, I had some bread and a pot of jam a French man had given me. The French were very good to us these times. A good many French wagons belonging to farmers were taken into use for carrying the sick etc.

The same day Monday the 31st found us lying in a wood performing the duties of flank guard to our force retiring. A very arduous job it was too, walking through the wood for hours and then out on the road through the forest. This was a very hot day and one of the worst for marching we had had as yet, so that it was a pity to see the poor chaps trudging along, and always the sound of guns firing behind us. It was a strange thing too that hardly one of the men believed we were getting beaten back, for our officers continually told us it was a strategical move we were doing, so as to surround the enemy. We did at times think it strange we had to go so fast, but we believed what they told us, and so it came to pass that we did eventually flank them and they were in their turn the pursued. It seemed marvellous to us how every morning after a trying night march we would find them on our heels again, but we found out that they came up on motor buses.'

18 The wheels and shaft of a gun carriage.

3
September 1914: Stand and Fight

Before dawn had broken on 1 September, the Battalion was on the move again towards Verberie. Here the Faughs were ordered to support the 19th Infantry Brigade to the north of Néry; however, the fighting was practically over by the time they arrived. At Néry they found out that earlier that day the 1st Cavalry Brigade, under Brigadier General C. J. Briggs, had been attacked, but had not only driven back the Germans but had also successfully captured two complete artillery batteries.

About 3pm, the retreat across country continued due south towards Rully, crossing the line of an ancient Roman road. The 10th Brigade was again acting as rearguard and would not reach its bivouac at Baron until after dark. It was another scorching hot day, and having to cross ploughed fields proved slow work for the horse-drawn transport. The hope of a good night's sleep was denied the Faughs, as they were allocated perimeter guard duty. Any annoyance was offset by the arrival of the first mail from home.

In the early hours of 2 September the retreat continued, and after another hot day's marching the

In the village of Néry are found several memorials marking the British cavalry victory that took place there on the misty morning of 1 September 1914. During this conclusive action 'L' Battery of the Royal Horse Artillery won three Victoria Crosses and helped win the Battle of the Marne for the British. The advancing German cavalry and artillery surprised the British, and in the first few minutes of the action 'L' Battery lost two guns, five officers and 49 men killed or wounded. Only five men were left to man the one remaining gun. Captain Bradbury VC, though mortally wounded, was propped up against the gun and continued to direct the firing of the gun by BSM Dorrell and Sgt Nelson, supplied with shells by Driver Osborne and Gunner Darbyshire. When the 1st Battalions of the Middlesex Regiment and the Scottish Rifles arrived and charged the enemy, they recovered the British guns and captured eight German guns. Captain Bradbury VC died of his wounds and is buried in Néry Communal graveyard.

The Faughs spent several days and nights sheltering in French apple orchards. Those in the Magny area have now been built over by Disneyland, Paris.

Faughs found themselves bivouacked in a pleasant orchard near the little town of Dammartin en Goele.

Before daylight the next day the march was resumed, the 10th Brigade again taking the role of rearguard. The hot and weary troops marched through Juilly, Claye-Souilly and Annet to Lagny; the latter was just 10 miles due east of Paris, the ultimate goal of the German Army. Here the River Marne was crossed as its bridges were being prepared for demolition and heavy guns hauled into position. The Faughs bivouacked in a stubble field to the south-east of the Bois de Chigny.

That night, for the first time in weeks, the Battalion had a full night's rest. The remainder of the day was spent in replacing lost equipment and clothing, due to the fighting and prolonged retreat. In the evening the Battalion moved to Magny-le-Hongres[19] and found themselves a good spot to spend the night in one of the many fruit orchards in the area. For the many men in the battalion from Armagh it must have been redolent of home, as Sgt Wilson describes:

> 'With a little rest that night, the next morning found us extended in artillery formation across a large space of country. This formation, which is a difficult one for artillery to deal with, we kept the whole day and retired a good distance. We heard that six guns had been captured by the Middlesex Regt, the German gunners being all killed and what was left taken prisoners. We rested when it grew dark and lay down on some straw, which was very comfortable.
>
> At 5 am the following morning we were off again and after another stiff march halted in a very pretty place called "Dan Martin"[20]. Here we found ourselves quartered in an orchard and found now that we were within 20 miles off Paris. However, we enjoyed one stay in the orchard, as all the fruit being ripe we appeased our hunger and also got a good meal and wash finishing up with a little rest. That night we were off again and did not stop until we were within 6 miles off Paris.
>
> We stayed however that day behind some cottages and for the first time did a little bit of squaring up, calling the roll and checking it, making casualty reports out etc. We spent a very pleasant day here, washing and resting ourselves. In the evening the Chaplain held a prayer meeting and all the French people gathered round to hear us singing.
>
> Friday the 4th Sept found us on the move again and off and on all day when we got leave to halt for the night and were lucky to get

[19] This is now the site of Disneyland, Paris.

[20] Dammartin en Goele

The Faughs bivouacked in an orchard in Dammartin en Goele on the night of 2/3 September 1914. Sgt Wilson thought it a very pretty village and the men appeased their hunger with the ripe apples.

It was at the village of Chevry near Paris that the Faughs stopped retreating, dug in and turned to face the German attack on 5 September 1914.

some nice straw to lie on. We did not get much sleep for there were constant alarms.'

In the early hours of 5 September Major A. R. Burrowes assumed command of the 1st Battalion and led the Faughs in the column heading south through Serris-Ferrières and the Forest d'Armainvillers to the village of Chevry, where for the Faughs the retreat from Mons stopped. As dawn broke they joined the rest of the 10th Brigade and took up their positions as part of the advance guard, now facing north and the Germans!

Also at Chevry, Lieutenant Penn was waiting with reinforcements, the first to arrive since the Battalion landed in France. These were men from the 3rd Special Reserve Battalion of the Faughs who, after a few weeks of intensive training at Dunree Fort in Co Donegal, volunteered for the BEF.

On the right of the British Expeditionary Force was the French Fifth Army, on its left the French Sixth Army. The latter badly needed the reinforcements that were waiting in Paris, in order to prevent that city from falling into German hands. In surprise and secrecy General Galliéni requisitioned every available lorry and 600 Paris Renault taxis (each carrying five men) to move an entire division into the field of battle. These fresh troops arriving in the nick of time, mounted a successful attack and pushed back the German right flank. Strategically this was to prove a crucial move in the Battle of the Marne, which was now commencing.

On the evening of 6 September in brilliant moonlight the Brigade was able to retrace its steps through the forest, following the route of the previous day and halting at Serris. The Faughs finally took up position to the west of Crecy. During that calm and quiet night the Faughs could hear for the first time the sounds of a German retreat.

After 'Stand To'[21] the next day the Faughs and the Royal Warwickshire Regiment were sent across the Grand Morin River to Ferrolles, to cover the troops crossing at Crecy. From here they advanced slowly towards Giremoutiers via Maisoncelles, where they bivouacked for the night.

A Royal Irish Fusilier soldier at 'Stand To'.

The enemy was in retreat across the Marne at La Ferté[22]. On 8 September the 10th Brigade, now in reserve, reached Petit Courrais by noon. The Battalion halted there for the night and the 10th Brigade established its HQ in l'Hotel des Bois. Here, among the debris of war, the Faughs found the discarded Cuirasses[23] of the French heavy cavalry, from which they derived their name; they had quickly found that this mediaeval chest armour was of little protection against the German Maxim machine gun. At Petit Courrais Lieutenant O'Donovan and 99 other ranks managed to catch up with the 1st Battalion; they had been missing since the Battle of Le Cateau when they had become separated from the main force.

Now commanders had the opportunity to submit recommendations for French gallantry awards for the Battle of Le Cateau. They were written while sheltering in a ditch by the roadside and handed to Brigade HQ, located under a cart in the farmyard.

The names of 20 Royal Irish Fusiliers on the La Ferté-sous-Jouarre Memorial.

---

[21] An Army term for a high state of alertness. It is usual Army practice when in the field to 'Stand To' for an hour either side of dawn and dusk, or at any time if an attack is imminent. In the trenches, 'Stand To' meant standing on the Firing Step with weapons ready to fire toward the enemy position. When the men were in the front-line trenches the daily rum ration was handed out after the dawn 'Stand To'.

[22] The memorial at La Ferté-sous-Jouarre commemorates those killed during the retreat from Mons and the Battle of the Aisne and Marne and who have no known grave. There are 20 Royal Irish Fusiliers on the Memorial.

[23] This was highly polished chest armour.

Above **The memorial at La Ferté-sous-Jouarre commemorates those soldiers killed during the early months of the war and who have no known grave.**

All those recommended received gallantry medals, including the author of this journal, Sgt Hugh Wilson:

> 'The next morning Saturday we were on the move by 3 am and marched from that until 1 pm when we bivouacked in a field. This day was very hot and it was here that our first reinforcements came in. We were pulled out of bed at half past two the next morning and kept on the move until 9 am when we stayed by a farmhouse. They were fighting pretty hard now just in front and we could see the ambulances bringing in the wounded and dead.
>
> Monday the 7th found us at Crecy and we now knew we were making a forward

Right **The Royal Irish Fusiliers shelter in a sunken road during the retreat from Mons amid the debris of war and retreating troops.**

movement. We halted on the outskirts of a deserted village and took up a position along side the road. It began to rain very heavy now and the majority of us had no coats but our shoulders were protected by our oil sheets which we tied round. It was very miserable lying here wet through almost and with nothing to do. We had the road in front barrackaded[24] and it was now dark so there was nothing to do only lie and wait.

Our attention was drawn to a noise up the road and as we looked we could see something white moving and later on we seen it was a large white horse belonging to some farmer. We thought we had a Ulan at first. I was at the head of the Battalion this time and so I caught hold of it and the CO told me to take the dam[25] thing out of it. So I thought it was a good chance to get a ride if we were going to do another long march which we were expecting. So I took him down to the rear of the Battn[26] and I got some abuse I can tell you, as the old horse was not particular where he put his big feet down, anyhow he trod on feet and ribs of about dozen on his way, that that I was glad when I reached the end of the Battalion. It was quite dark and I was getting him hopelessly mixed up amongst the transport.

The order then came to move and so I put my rifle round his neck and started to get on. He knocked me off the first time he was so high. I succeeded in the finish by climbing on a wagon first and holding him alongside. So I rode on and I began to think I had backed a winner, but no – the second in command came alongside. I suppose he took me for a general, anyhow he said the horse would be very useful for riding for a man who had sore feet and so I had to put him up and then lead the horse. I didn't want any more of that so the next morning I asked a Frenchman to give me five francs for him, but he must have thought he was too dear. I tied him to a fence and the last of him I saw was the cook Sgt had him tied to his wagon.

To go on, I was warned now to take over the duties of machine gun Sergeant as the other Sergeant had been lost, so I bid goodbye to my platoon and wended my way to the machine gun section. The Dublins had a bit of luck with their guns sometime previously, smashing up a number of the enemy who had come too close.

We now got on the move again, marching in an easterly direction. I found now that marching was made a little easier for me as I could now put my pack on the limber. We now heard that we were moving east for a flank attack on the enemy who was marching on Paris. In this, our Brigade was held in Reserve, for in the previous fighting we had been at the front. Shell fire now could be heard in the front and we afterwards heard we had been successful in driving them back and in capturing 40 guns.

On Wednesday the 9th we were still in reserve, but we were expecting to be called on any minute, as the troops in our front were heavily engaged. Word was now passed that the enemy were retiring and I need not say how pleased we all were, but sorry to have given a hand in this. The gun fire could be heard receding and we felt quite joyful, and as we went on past Jouarre.'

In the early evening of 9 September the 10th Brigade was on the move again towards Les Poupelains. Lieutenant G. M. H. Wright rejoined the Battalion from his staff appointment, and it was about this time that the service postcard was first taken into widespread use. It proved hugely successful and was seldom misused, although the non-commissioned officer who sent one to all his friends with all sentences stroked out except 'I have not received your parcel' was considered not to be playing the game.

24 Sgt Wilson's spelling

25 Damn

26 Battalion

The following morning the Brigade crossed the Marne via the railway bridge at Le Saussoy without opposition. The only major problem was dragging the heavy supply wagons across the railway lines. As they continued they passed through Dhuisy and Coulombs to Hervillers. Evidence of the enemy's hasty retreat were half-consumed rations left in ransacked houses.

By 11 September the 10th Brigade was now the advance guard. Its route lay through the Bois de Gandelu[27], but the track quickly became a forest path and the remainder of the troops were diverted to the west of the forest. A few prisoners, some wounded, were picked up, but no active resistance was found in the woods. On emerging at St Quentin the vanguard found itself on the same road as the 5th Division. The French Turcos[28] were now on the left flank and their quaint dress was a novelty to the Irishmen. The Faughs now began to come across widespread evidence of the German retreat. Abandoned wagons and equipment lay everywhere and there were many graves of hastily buried bodies.

On 10 September 1914 the 10th Brigade hauled its heavy supply wagons up the steep banks and across the lines of the railway bridge at Le Saussoy.

A forest track through the Bois de Gandelu near Chouy. On 11 September 1914 the Faughs found several wounded German prisoners in this large wood.

[27] This is now called Bois de Montigny. The Faughs split their force in order to both move through and make a flanking movement to the west of the forest, thereby catching any German stragglers. They came out the other side and down a forest track and reunited on the road to St Quentin.

[28] The Turcos were raised in Algeria of mostly native Arabic and Turkish troops. They wore white trousers and an embroidered blue jacket topped by a red fez or white turban. They earned a reputation for brutality and extreme savagery on the field of battle.

The march continued via Passy-en-Valois, across the River Ourcq to Chouy. Here there had been some fierce fighting and the first dead civilians were seen. After marching through heavy rain it was a comfort to shelter in the large farm of La Loge[29], the first time the Battalion had been under cover since landing in the country. The accommodation proved surprisingly comfortable.

La Loge Farm at Chouy where the Faughs spent their first night under cover since landing in France.

The Royal Irish Fusilier officers slept on the kitchen floor of La Loge farmhouse and the soldiers slept in the haylofts and barns.

[29] This farm still stands in a commanding position on top of the ridge by the road from Chouy to Louatre. The officers slept on the kitchen floor and the soldiers in the haylofts and barns. This was their first night under cover since the 1st Battalion had landed at Boulogne. In 1914 the farm was called La Loge Tristan and was owned by Monsieur Ferte and his family. When Ferte was killed during the Second World War his widow sold the farm to its present owners, Gilbert and Christianne Grymonprez. Although the farmhouse is now much smaller owing to fire damage, the interior would still be recognisable by the Faughs. Indeed, the decorative floor tiles in the family room still show the damage caused by the rough boots and equipment of either the British or German soldiers. Monsieur Grymonprez, originally from Belgium, found the barrel of a British Lee Enfield .303 rifle when he was clearing out a drainage ditch close to the farmhouse; it is easy to envisage that a battle-damaged rifle would be judged safely discarded in the drainage ditch of a remote farm. Monsieur and Madame Grymonprez very kindly and generously donated this memento of the Faughs' sojourn at La Loge Farm to the Royal Irish Fusiliers Museum.

Sgt Wilson continues:

'The 2nd reinforcements came in on Thursday we were at La Ferté and only marched about seven miles. This day we heard of no engagement with any harm. At night we got good quarters in a shed with plenty of straw to lie in, but had to move early as by 4 am we had limbered up and were on the move. This time we were advance guard and passed through a place called Chouy or Chorry. The Germans were getting very severely handled as they retired as their traces shown.

There were whole packs of artillery shells left, the whole place was strewn with dead horses and the smell was awful, as the weather was very hot again. We passed several of their trenches, and they had had no time to remove their dead for they were lying about all over. One halt we got by the road, we sat down on some straw in the ditch by the side and one chap thought it felt funny and so turned it up, when he found it full of dead bodies. We soon shifted I can tell you.

We stayed in a school room this night, but it was not so comfortable as the small desks made no room for lying down. Anyhow, we could not sleep, so I started to explore and succeeded in finding in a cellar a good supply of all kinds of wine and out at the back some eggs. So we passed the time as well we could, cooking and having a little meal. I found a lovely bicycle outside, but as there was no way to take it, I had to leave it. At 5 am we were getting ready to move for now I had to see to getting the guns, ammunition and limber ready and the horses in, so by 6 am we were on the move again.'

The 10th Brigade was once again the advance guard. To the sound of an artillery barrage they marched by Louatre and Villemontoire to Septmonts. Both British and French armies were in close contact, the nearest troops to the 10th Brigade being the Chasseurs d'Afrique. On reconnaissance duties these light cavalry troopers, resplendent in their sky-blue uniforms and mounted on grey horses, proved their worth.

At approximately 4.30pm the advance guard was drawn up on the ridge north of Septmonts overlooking the Aisne valley. The entire 10th Brigade cheered when the 4th Division's 60-pounder batteries opened fire on the retreating Germans. To many it recalled the scene from the

The ridge at Septmonts overlooking the Aisne valley. As the German Army retreated over this ridge the 10th Brigade cheered as the British artillery found their target. In the middle distance can be seen the turrets of Septmonts chateau; this was destroyed during the artillery duel and the damage caused by both British and German artillery can still be seen.

top of Talana Hill in South Africa on the evening of 20 October 1899[30]. They marched through pouring rain, eventually finding welcome shelter at Septmonts after dark.

On the night of 12/13 September the 4th Division were the first Allied troops to fight their way across the River Aisne, seizing Bucy-le-Long and the heights to the north. By this time the 10th Brigade was allowed to rest in the reserve of the advance guard and moved slowly via Billy-sur-Aisne, ending up in a covered position adjacent to La Tuilerie, where it waited for some time. The only excitement was the sound of German shells whizzing overhead. As night fell the 1st Battalion crossed the Aisne by the damaged bridge at Venisel and spent a cold wet night bivouacked in the open. The Battle of the Aisne continued the next day while the 1st Battalion was deployed on the southern side of Bucy-le-Long.

During the battle the troops had become hopelessly intermingled. The Faughs were called to give support in several different positions and as a result suffered more from shellfire than those troops actually in the front line, who at least had the protection of trenches and caves.

The Faughs fell prey to the searching fire from the German howitzer batteries. These massive guns, of 8.1-inch calibre, were known as 'Crumps', 'Black Marias', or 'Woolly Bears'. On 17 September the Battalion lost heavily in men and horses to these guns, Lieutenant and Quartermaster Bunting DCM and Company Sergeant Major Fynne being among those wounded. During the closing days of September the Battalion was employed in various duties, guarding bridges, clearing the battlefield of the dead and working on trenches.

It was also at this time that the Kaiser's famous order was read by the British troops: 'It is my Royal and Imperial command that you concentrate your energies for the immediate present upon one single purpose, and that is that you address all your skill and all the valour of my soldiers to exterminate first the treacherous English; walk over General French's Contemptible little Army.' This term of derision was seized upon by the soldiers of the British Expeditionary Force and, in the years after the war, 'the Old Contemptibles' became a badge of honour.

Warfare has always been the catalyst for innovation and invention, and the BEF was quick to put new ideas into action. By the end of the second month of the war the first anti-aircraft gun

The Aisne east of Soissons where the 4th Division were the first Allied troops to fight their way across the river.

[30] On that date during the Boer War the Faughs were pinned down by the Boers on the steep slopes of Talana Hill, near Dundee. The Faughs advanced, led by Capt Burrowes (who also fought with the 1st Battalion during the Great War and later wrote *The 1st Battalion the Faugh a Ballaghs in the Great War*), but suffered heavy casualties. When at last the British artillery found their range, the Boers started to take many casualties and were forced to retreat. But the cavalry did not follow up the infantry's success and, as at Septmonts, the enemy escaped and the Faughs were forced to leave the ground for which they had paid such a heavy price, and march away in the pouring rain.

was made by putting a pom-pom light gun on a cartwheel. This was secured to the floor of a wagon and could be spun round to whichever direction the aircraft were flying from. To boost morale and unity among the troops, daily intelligence summaries were made available and were avidly read by all ranks.

The Battalion had proved its fitness, with only seven men admitted to hospital in September, despite the fact that during the retreat and advance the men had marched 260 miles in 22 days without a rest. Sgt Wilson's journal continues:

> 'The enemy was reported to be at Soissons and we could hear the artillery of both sides hard at it. The French were on our left and our 5th Division was on the right. This day turned out very wet and we had no rations. We had great difficulty crossing the River Marne as the bridge was almost destroyed and we had to cross by the railway bridge and the wagons had to be man-handled across. We spent a very miserable night in the rain and next day was much brighter, we were moving all day off and on that is with halts here and there. At these halts we could get generally plenty of apples and damsons which grew in abundance. It was as well we did get it, for if it had not been for fruit the last few days we would have fared ill.
>
> Sunday night the 13th of Sept found us crossing the Aisne by means of a Pontoon bridge put across by our engineers and the engineers suffered rather heavily during this as they were under fire the whole time. Before we came to this bridge we were resting in a hollow amongst the woods, and we came again under shell fire. I got my back to a tree and the others got about the limber so that none of us were hit. The Germans were doing now what we had previously done, that was destroying the bridges on their retreat. We crossed over safely, only the artillery lost one gun whilst going over. It was afterwards regained I think.
>
> During this march by night the artillery was going the whole time and they were bursting on all sides of us. We were now marching across the valley, the Germans being in position on the heights across the valley. It now commenced to rain and so it did not improve our spirits. To our left as we advanced the town of Soissons could be plainly seen as it was all lit up owing to parts of it being on fire and no wonder for the Germans were showing their hate by crashing them in it as fast as they could. We arrived eventually at the foot of the hill and stayed the night in a little village named Bucy-le-Long.
>
> Monday the 14th found us still lying under the slope of the hill with the artillery firing very heavy on both sides. I went round the village during the day and found the houses had been turned topsy turvey by the Germans. It was a shame the way they had ransacked some beautiful houses. There was plenty of grapes about so I had a good feed. The order now came that the machine guns were to be brigaded, that is all together under one officer and so like this we went up the hill and going up was awful, especially with us carrying guns and ammunition, the hill was so steep. We had to take cover several times as the shelling was so severe. However we managed to reach the top without losing any of our men.
>
> We now came to a large farm house with walls all round and so round these walls we crept. The officer pointed a haystack out as a good position, but changed his mind and did not send us. It was as well for we would have all been done in going to it. The ground round about was being literally torn up with shells. The Seaforth Battalion was on our right and they were loosing heavily, the men being brought in, in dozens. Our officer took us round the other side of the farm and there we saw another haystack, so we decided to make for it, and with a bit of dodging succeeded in reaching it, where we began to dig a trench behind, and there we remained until night. When dusk came on we went back to the farm house and found a nice place to sleep in a barn. We brought our limbers in with us. The farmer and his staff were still in the house and our Officers made their abode with them.
>
> We found that the Seaforths had lost their

Commanding Officer and another officer also. I saw them both before they were buried and they looked very peaceful. The Chaplain asked me if I could let him have a couple of blankets to bury them in, but we had only the one each and he said it did not matter as the living had to be thought about first. I find that afterwards they found a coffin in the village below and so gave him a decent burial. There was one poor chap of the Seaforths lying in the room of the house and he had got an awful wound in the back, poor chap, we could see he had not long to live for he was swimming in blood.

The next day at dawn we resumed our position by the haystack and it was fairly quiet for us and we returned at night to the farm house again. The artillery fire was pretty close but did not manage to catch us. This night there was a proper fusillade of rifle fire for about an hour, and the rifle bullets rained over. We quietened down eventually and had a good nights rest, but at the dawn the following morning the artillery fire broke out again and continued nearly the whole day. This sort of thing occurred every day now for some time until we finally left the position.

One day as I was on top of a haystack close by the gun, I could see the enemy's trenches quite plain and could see them reading newspapers and giving rations out. I noticed as I was up there, 5 men coming towards our position, they were not many hundreds of yards away. I was just going to have a pop at them when I thought if I hit one the rest would perhaps get away before I hit another. So I sent word to the Company in the trenches in front, who according to the ground could not see them. They went out on a patrol and captured them.

Instead now of making our headquarters at the farm during the night, we were told off to go into the trenches of the Seaforths with our guns, and so every night at dusk we would leave the haystack and go to the trenches, coming away at dawn. It was lovely weather

Lt Furness and the Seaforth Highlanders in the front-line trenches above Bucy-le-Long.

now and we enjoyed our work, only the brightness was taken off it, by someone every day almost getting killed.

The Battalion, during this time, was lying in reserve at the bottom of the hill, but they were just in as bad a position as we if not worse. They got a severe shelling while in the village, when the whole village was completely wrecked. We lost a good number of men this day, one a Sgt friend of mine who I felt the loss of very much. They were moved after this a little more up the slope of the hill, but were not then out of it, as the shrapnel found them occasionally.

The farm I was in with my section, seemed to escape wonderfully, men occasionally getting killed and wounded within its walls. I remember I had a near shave while in the barn. I was shaving and whilst I was, the shells were just grazing the back wall and going over on to our Battalion below. The barn was just at the back wall and I never thought they would change but just skim over the wall above us. Anyhow I had the glass on the back of the door and had just bent down to the bucket, when one burst just outside at the door. When the smoke had gone, I saw just above the glass a large hole blown in the door. It was a good job I had not my head there or I think some of it would have been missing. One chap out in the yard got the rim of his cap cut completely off without injuring him a bit. Another poor chap got his inside blew out and we buried him at night.

We were surprised one day to see hundreds of cattle drinking in the yard and wondered where they had come from and we found that the place was a mass of underground caves in which they were all sheltered. Our artillery made use of these afterwards for their horses, and by the trenches of the Seaforths, were another lot in which the whole Battalion could have gone inside. There was no fear of a Jack Johnson[31] finding you here.

I got a good shot with the gun one day when by the haystack. As usual we used to observe from the top of the haystack where we used to bury ourselves in the straw. The enemy used to walk about freely enough about their trenches, as there was a rise of ground between they and us. This day however they seemed to have collected together a little more, as far as I could see someone was reading a paper to them. I decided to teach them to be a little more careful and so putting one of our men on the haystack with glasses to watch, I laid the gun. As I could not see them I took my bearing, and laid on the crest with a little additional elevation. When I had it laid I saw that if I fired the bullets would pass within a few feet of the head of the man on the haystack, so I told him but he said he would chance it, he must have trusted my shooting. I was not so bad at it, being the best shot in the Battalion. Anyhow when he gave me the signal, I blazed off and as he told me it was great to see them skip. You wouldn't see a head inside half a minute. They kept a little lower in future.

No matter what position we took up it seemed the enemy knew all about it, and no wonder for numbers of spies were caught behind our lines. The old chap in the farm it afterwards turned out was a spy. He was caught communicating to them by wire in one of the caves. We had often wondered how it was our house escaped and now we knew. It's an ill wind that blows nobody any good they say, and so it was with us for had it not been so we would have been all blown up long ago.

We were awfully hard up for cigarettes now and if we could occasionally get a bit of tobacco of a Frenchman we would make cigarettes of any paper we could get, but soon after this we got cigarettes from home and were pleased I can tell you. In the line of rations we got the best and sometimes double and they now commenced to give us a small issue of rum. The CO below told them to send us up the best as we were the only ones in the

[31] This heavy German shell was named after Jack Johnson, a contemporary champion heavyweight boxer.

Battalion that was doing anything, having been in the firing line all the time. But the Battalion got it as bad as us, for the shells that went too far always dropped on them.

The same thing continued now, artillery fire all day, then we would go to the other trenches at night, but going up to the haystack in the morning used to be a terror, we had to fairly run the gauntlet. One of our gunners, we used to put behind a wall at the top of an old barn, but he was changed and one of the Warwicks Regt went there. He wasn't there one hour before the wall was blown down and he was badly blown about. He died shortly afterwards.

On Sunday the 20th Sept we were as usual by evening in the trenches and an attack was repulsed. It was quite exciting while it lasted. We could not see much in front, only the bullets were coming in and so we blazed away with rifles and machine guns for all we were worth. We had barbed wire out in front and big holes dug all over to trip them up, but they did not get that far.'

4
October 1914: THE FIRST TRENCHES

On 1 October the Faughs took over the right flank of the 10th Brigade from the King's Own and the Essex Regiments. The men were relieved when they found that the latter's trenches were in exceptionally good shape. The line of trenches to the north of St Marguerite was held as follows: 'B' Company on the right, 'D' Company on the left, 'A' Company in support to the rear, the Machine Gun Section on the right of 'A' Company, with 'C' Company on detached duty, guarding bridges.

The enemy trenches were plainly visible about three-quarters of a mile in front. The German shelling was fairly continuous, but owing to deep trenches and the configuration of the ground, Faugh casualties were light. For the men, life in the trenches was a pleasant change from all the marching and they gladly put a lot of effort into improving them.

Battalion HQ was in a ruined house under the brow of a hill and it was here that the Faughs' French interpreter, Sergeant Henri B. de la Rancheraye, 24th Regiment Territorials, cooked one of the best meals the headquarters staff had tasted for a long time.

On 4 October Regimental Sergeant Major Murphy was commissioned as a Second Lieutenant. This was the first such field promotion in the Faughs, but it would not be the last. The need for officers was so great that, in the first month of the war alone, the British Army commissioned 500 Warrant Officers and NCOs. Countless more would follow during the next four years.

Sgt Wilson continues his story:

> 'We carried on like this until Friday, October 2nd, when our Battalion came up and we joined them in the trenches. We had moved to the right about half a mile, and were established in good trenches. We used to knock about pretty openly in these trenches, but one day, while up looking at something a shell nearly took our caps off, so we kept a little lower in future. Down at the bottom of the hill was a little village[32] and the little church had been used as a hospital, for the place was full of damaged rifles and bayonets and the pews were all stained with blood. I changed my bayonet here as my own was damaged. The one I got had a little blood on it but it was almost new.
>
> On Saturday the 3rd we received a paper for the first time[33] and it was dated the 1st. We also got gifts of cigarettes and books from friends at home, so we began to get along quite nicely now. I had a nice little dugout made but I could not lie full length in it as it was so short. Divine Service was now kept and nearly all attended, for men who had never prayed before went and prayed now. The aeroplanes now began to trouble us a lot, showing by means of signals our position, with the result

[32] This was probably Venisel.

[33] Mrs Douglas Churcher, whose husband had served with the Faughs during the Boer War, organised gifts and comforts to be sent to the Royal Irish Fusiliers and also arranged for W. H. Smith & Sons to send newspapers.

The church (now rebuilt) at Venisel was used as a hospital in October 1914.

we would get shelled and would have to lie in the bottom of the trench. The shells as a rule did little damage only when they fired behind us they would generally kill a few horses.'

The 10th Brigade made an early start on 7 October and marched through Septmonts and Rozières, where they passed the graves of Faughs who had been killed earlier in the fighting. The Battalion reached its billets at Hartennes about 7am. Here two blankets were issued to each man, together with two country carts to carry them. By 8pm the Brigade was again on the move, marching during the hours of darkness to avoid enemy observation from the air.

At 2am on 8 October the Brigade arrived at Rozet St Albin, having marched through Oulchy-la-Ville. There was a short rest before continuing at 4.30am. The Brigade passed through Chouy again before halting for two hours at Ancienville, which gave the men time to cook a meal.

When the march recommenced the 10th Brigade passed through Dampleux Pisseleux before reaching the *sucerie* (sugar factory) at Vauciennes in the early hours of 9 October. At 4.15pm the march continued via Crepy-en-Valois to Rully, arriving at 10pm. Here the Faughs were billeted in two large farms. At 3pm the next day the Battalion marched via Raray to another rest stop at Verberie. On 11 October the Battalion boarded a troop train at Longueil St Marie and proceeded via Creil, Amiens, Abbeville, Etaples, Boulogne and Calais to St Omer, where the men arrived in the early hours of 12 October.

The journal describes the events:

> 'We had now been in this position for over three weeks so when on Tuesday the 6th October we got our marching orders we were all pleased, for we know we would get something more lively to do. So at night we handed our trenches over to the French Alpines and moved off. We marched a good distance and billeted in a village in Aisne. We remained under cover all day and the following night found us travelling again. We marched through the night and towards dawn got a good billet and remained there all day.
>
> The next night, Thursday, we got a pretty stiff march over 20 miles and on Friday morning marched into the town of Villers, we were all billeted in a large sugar factory. The French here had a large aeroplane shed and we spent a good deal of the day watching them go out and come in. In the evening we set off again and got to Villers where our detachment got quartered in a dance room. We had a nice time here and got on well with the French who gave us the use of their cooking utensils. We could also get plenty of eggs as we went along so that we did very well. We also received letters now regularly and despatched them whenever we got the chance.
>
> We got on the move again, and after marching some time we again got quartered in a small loft above an inn. There were a party

of English who left the inn while we were there for home. At 3 pm we left for the station to entrain. There was not much accommodation for travelling on this train as there were so many of us. We got our machine gun limbers mounted on an open truck and as there was no room in the carriages for us we got up on the truck with the guns. It was nice weather and so it was very pleasant riding out in the open, only a bit rotten when we went under any tunnels. We came out black as a rule. We went by way of Boulogne and got a good reception on the stations as we travelled along, getting all sorts of gifts given us. The girls were very keen on our badges and buttons and if we had given them all they wanted we would have left ourselves stripped.

We eventually arrived at St Omer where we detrained and found quarters in a gymnasium and chapel. The Battalion remained while we left earlier with the transport. It was a good long march and we were glad when we got to the end. There was no billet for us and so we made shift for ourselves.'

By now the weather had turned bitterly cold and due to the inexperience of the officers in charge at the station the detraining at St Omer was a shambles. The Battalion was billeted at the College de St Joseph for several hours and at noon marched to the Grande Place, to join the rest of the 10th Brigade, which was waiting for the French motor buses that would take it to Hazebrouck. Before the buses could arrive a German aeroplane dropped its load of bombs on the assembled men, causing many casualties. Luckily for the Faughs, rather than just standing around waiting in the Grande Place, they had taken the opportunity to go to the nearby church and attend Mass.[34]

At daybreak on 13 October, after a night spent on the French buses, which had eventually turned up, the Battalion found itself in the neighbourhood of Hazebrouck. After a short rest and some food, they marched on, passing through Caestre and arriving

On 12 October 1914 the Faughs marched through the Grande Place at St Omer to go to Mass in the church near the Square. The church spire can be seen in the background.

[34] A letter from Pte J. Connoly to his mother in Armagh was published in the *Armagh Guardian* on 20 November 1914: 'Just a few lines to thank you for the Testament. It is very nice to have one out here as there is no chance of us getting to church, but we see plenty of them. We have time to write now and again, but we never know if we shall get blown to pieces or not...'

A letter from Cpl Toal to his mother in Cork was published in the *News of the World* on 29 November 1914: 'The thing that we mind more than anything else is not being able to get to Mass. Time and again we have wanted to go, if only to say a couple of prayers for the souls of our comrades killed by the barbarians. One officer – he's a Protestant himself – told us it was very hard lines on us, for the Germans seemed always to know when we were setting out for chapel and began fighting to stop us. I fancy they must think we fight better after we have been to Mass...'

at Flêtre at 1pm. At 2.25pm orders were received to attack, and the Battalion moved to its rendezvous on the first by-road leading north-east of Flêtre.

The Germans were holding an entrenched position running north and south through Méteren. The attack was to be made by the 4th Division in the centre, with the 6th Division on its right flank and Allenby's Cavalry Division on the left. The Faughs' specific objective was the farm at Fontaine-Houck and an area running 660 yards south of the farm. The Seaforths were on the right and the Royal Dublin Fusiliers on the left flank.

The 1st Battalion dispositions were as follows: 'C' Company (Sgt Wilson's company) commanded by Captain Carbery on the right, 'D' Company commanded by Captain Incledon-Webber on the left, 'A' Company commanded by Captain Kavanagh in support, and 'B' Company commanded by Captain Bull on the left rear.

At 3.15pm the assault was launched through an afternoon mist that prevented effective artillery support. Within a few minutes heavy rain began to fall, turning the fields into a morass of mud. The men used their groundsheets to try and keep their rifles clean as their advance across the countryside was hampered by thick hedgerows. In these conditions moving consistently in the right direction was difficult, but nevertheless by nightfall the Faughs had captured the ridge north of Méteren. During the early stages of the fighting Lieutenant A. M. Samuels was hit and died of his wounds during the night.

Map showing the area around Méteren.

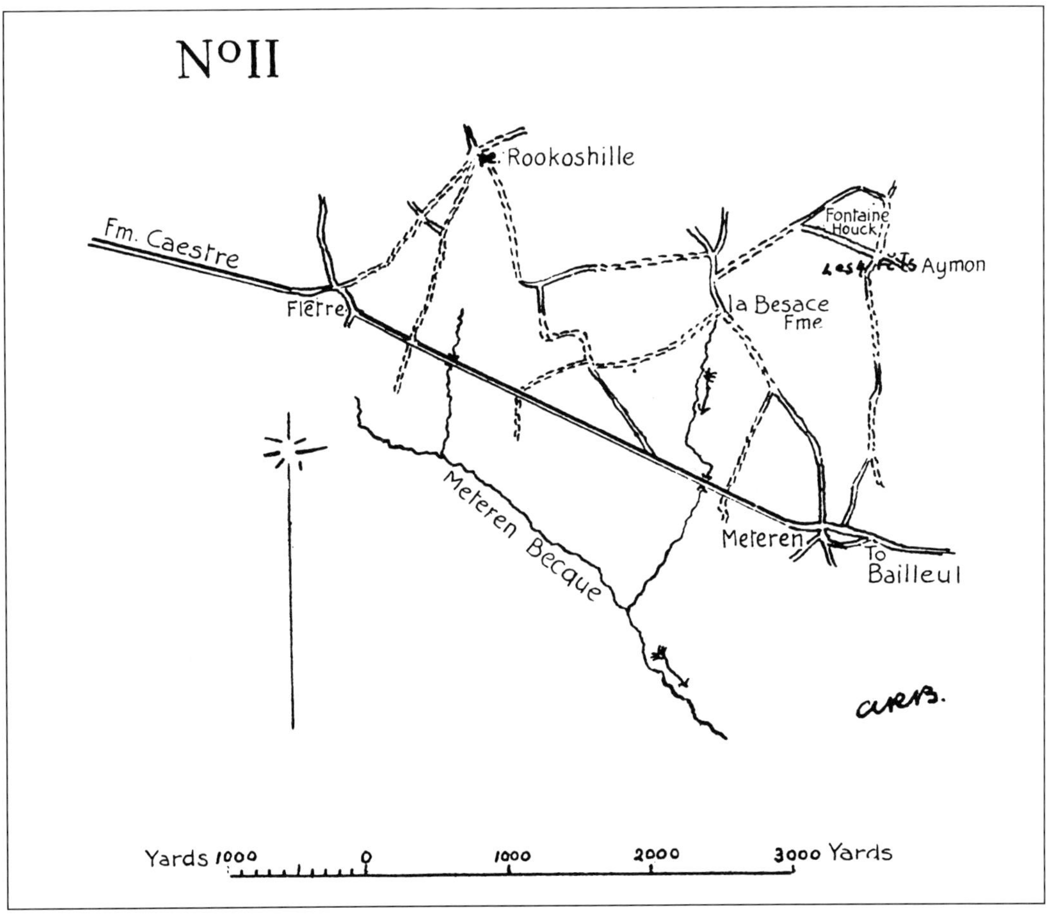

The slope leading up to the ridge north of Méteren. Although today the hedgerows have gone, the fields are still muddy. In the right background the spire of Méteren church can be seen. During the battle for the village and the ridge, the Germans occupied the spire, and observed from it. The Faughs captured the ridge and suffered several casualties, including Lt Arthur M. Samuels, who died of his wounds and is buried at Méteren Military Cemetery.

Back to Sgt Wilson's journal:

'On the following day, Tuesday the 13th Oct we could see that we had been brought to do a bit of active work, for now once more, after having a few days of quietness we could hear the guns again in action. We soon got our orders and got to know the enemy was holding a strong position in front of a town called Méteren. As we advanced up the hill we could hear the maxims[35] going. When we got to the summit the Battalion was extended for the attack and our officer chose his own way forward, as he had to get guns and limbers into a position that would be safe.

It was a little misty and so we could not see to fire, but the bullets were whistling by now pretty hot. We managed to get along by hedges until we were fairly close, when our artillery came into action. We with our guns did not manage this time to get into action as it being misty we could not see any aiming point, but we kept close on the heels of the Battalion. As we got close to them the fire was hot, but our chaps fixed bayonets and charged up the hill, they however did not wait for them but fled, leaving their dead behind them and so ended the day with our men in their trenches.

We lost pretty heavily crossing an open

[35] In 1885 the American inventor Hiram Maxim demonstrated the world's first automatic portable machine gun to the British Army. Maxim used the energy of each bullet's recoil force to eject the spent cartridge and insert the next bullet. The Maxim Machine Gun would therefore fire until the entire belt of bullets was used up. Trials showed that the machine-gun could fire 500 rounds per minute and therefore had the firepower of about 100 rifles. The Maxim Machine Gun was adopted by the British Army in 1889, and the following year the Austrian, German, Italian, Swiss and Russian armies also purchased Maxim's gun. It was first used by Britain's colonial forces in the Matabele war in 1893-94: in one engagement 50 soldiers fought off 5,000 Matabele warriors with just four Maxim guns. While in 1912 the British Army transferred its loyalties to the Vickers Gun and the lighter Lewis Gun, the German Army produced its own version of the Maxim. However, in the First World War several of the minor European armies continued to use the Maxim Gun.

Lt Arthur Samuels's grave at Méteren.

piece of ground, the Seaforth Regt and Warwicks losing the most. We lost a young officer[36] and he, along with other men, were buried the next morning. The Warwicks were unfortunate in having a company almost completely cut up by machine gun fire. The Germans had occupied a church spire for their guns as we afterwards found out. This night as we lay across the barricaded road we could hear the wounded crying out and the men were looking for them to bring them in. As we, with our limbers and guns were following the Battalion, we would have to stay occasionally and I and the officer would go on in front. It was at one of these that we nearly went too far for a shower of bullets meeting us at the corner. We managed to get on though for the road was clear only for a dead horse, but we had no time to start dragging it out of the way, so we rode horses, limbers and all over it.

When we were halted on the road for the night, there were a few houses and they were being used for the wounded. The woman of one had had her husband taken away by the Germans and locked up in a cellar. We went and got him out for her, he had been in without anything for two days. One of our boys going up the road found a German officer hiding in a ditch and collared him.'

On 14 October, a dull day; time was spent in deepening the trenches and carrying up more ammunition. While some of the men were frying some bacon for breakfast, the smell brought an NCO of the 1st Bavarian Regiment from his hiding place in a nearby culvert; it was later discovered that he had been on a reconnaissance mission. That evening the Faughs were moved into billets in Méteren, with the men sleeping in the local church, probably the same one used by the Germans so devastatingly as a machine gun post.

The following evening the 10th Brigade moved to billets in Bailleul, the Faughs again staying in the local church. Within its dimly lit aisles some men prayed, while others got on with their usual chores. The first honours awarded to the Regiment were published in 4th Divisional Orders: the Legion of Honour Croix de Chevalier was given to Second Lieutenant W. H. Liesching, and the Medaille Militaire to CSM Scrafield, CSM R. Neville, Sgt H. A. Wilson (author of the Journal), and Drummer Corrigan.

On 16 October the Faughs marched the short distance to new billets in farms east of La Crèche. At 6.45am on 17 October the Battalion formed the advance guard of the 10th Brigade, with 'B' Company under Captain Bull on the vanguard. The crossing of the River Lys at Erquinghem was slow due to the crowds of refugees on the roads. At 8.30am 'C' Company, led by Captain Carbery,

[36] This was Samuels. He was from Kingstown, Dublin, and was aged 25 when he died. He is buried at Méteren Military Cemetery.

The burnt-out farmhouse known as 'Sydney Street'. The Germans established a defensive position in this farmhouse; frustrated at the Germans' refusal to surrender, and his own casualties, Captain Kentish set the house on fire with the Germans still in it.

The Cemetery at Farm Phillipeaux, or 'Sydney Street', in 1924, with the debris of the old farmhouse in the background. Those who were killed here were buried close by, and their graves were later moved to one of the larger cemeteries in Houplines.

reinforced 'B', and by 9.30am the complete Battalion was acting as advance guard, ably supported by the Royal Dublin Fusiliers.

As part of the battle to take Armentières, around noon 'C' Company, led by Captain Carbery, rushed the Farm Phillipeaux at La Ruage. When Captain Carbery was mortally wounded, Captain Elkan took immediate command and continued the attack on the farm, which was set on fire. The farm was held by a detachment of Saxon infantry who refused to surrender and fought on in the flames, and several lives were lost attempting to rescue the wounded soldiers from the burning buildings. Two of these were Lance Corporal E. McCarthy and Private J. Murrogh – many of McCarthy's comrades believed he should have received the Victoria Cross.

In an attempt to save his men and to end the fight, Captain Kentish used his initiative, and found a party of Engineers to blow in the side of the farm building nearest to the road. Kentish then led the Faughs into the attack assisted by Lieutenant Corblet of the French Navy, who received the Military Cross for this action. By late evening all the defenders were killed. Within the Battalion this action became known as 'Sydney Street'.[37]

[37] The Siege of Sydney Street had taken place in London in January 1911 when a number of heavily armed Russian communist anarchists, who had tried to rob a jewellery shop, were cornered in a block of flats at 100 Sydney Street. With the police out-gunned, the then Home Secretary, Winston Churchill, called in the Army. Subsequently the anarchists set the block of flats on fire and died in the blaze.

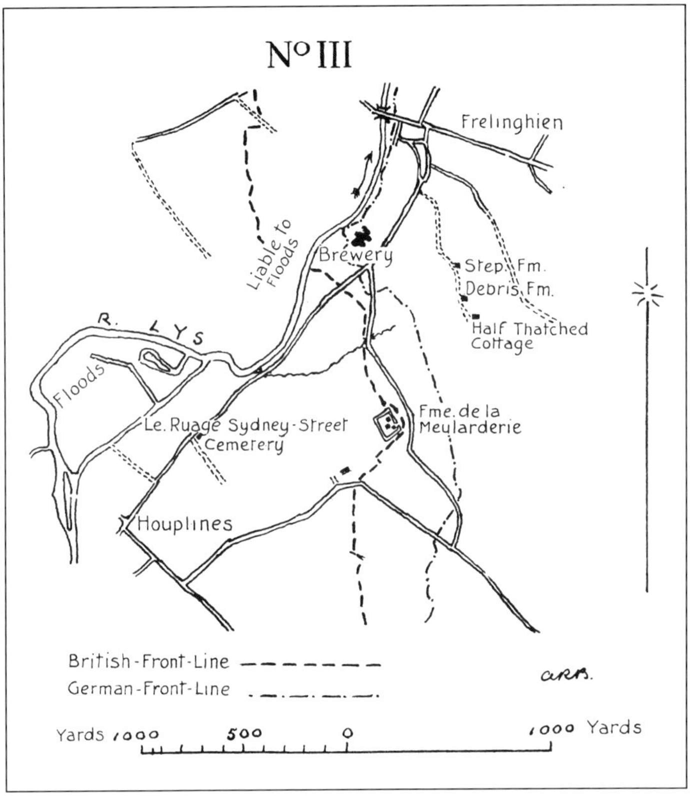

Map showing the area around 'Sydney Street' farmhouse near Houplines.

The grave of Sgt D. C. Jones DCM at Cité Bonjean Military Cemetery.

In recognition of their actions and bravery, Captain Kentish received the Distinguished Service Order, while Sergeant D. C. Jones and Privates L. Barton and B. Leddy received the Distinguished Conduct Medal, and Pte F. McKenna received the Russian Medal of St George.[38]

By noon Armentières was in British hands, but concealed German snipers continued to cause casualties for days afterwards until they were all rooted out. As night fell Captain Hill and 'D' Company had fought their way to Pont Ballot Farm; 'B' Company was on their left, having linked with 'C' Company at Le Ruage. They were ordered to hold on to all the ground they had gained. During the fighting at Pont Ballot Farm Captain Wright was severely wounded and owed his life to Private John Copeland, a Reservist of the Regiment, who carried him to safety under extreme enemy fire. Private Copeland was one of the first

[38] The citation for the DSO awarded to Captain Reginald John Kentish states that he, 'On October 17th 1914 set fire to a farm building occupied by some Germans, who had killed and wounded many of the attacking party. It was then found that some of the wounded lying close to the door were suffering from burning debris. He organised a rescue party, and himself, at the range of a few feet, endeavoured by firing down the passage, to keep down the fire of the occupants whilst the wounded were being removed.'

The citations for the DCMs awarded to Sgt D. C. Jones and Privates Barton and Leddy are the same and read as follows: 'For conspicuous gallantry on October 17th 1914 near Houplines, in volunteering to rescue under heavy fire some wounded men who were lying close to the door of a burning house held by the enemy. They were successful in recovering one wounded man.' Of the four, only Pte Barton survived the war.

Private Bernard Leddy DCM is pictured at the extreme right of the back row in the Battalion football team in 1912.

private soldiers of the Battalion to be mentioned in despatches during the war.[39]

Sgt Wilson continues:

'We rested here at Hazebrouck until 5 pm on Thursday, our Coys[40] being entrenched a little higher up the hill. During the day the officer and I went round the position previously occupied by the enemy and we wondered how it was possible for us to have come across such an open valley. If we had been in same position as the Germans they would never have driven us out. During the day the dead were buried, and some months later during a rest we had, we got the opportunity of visiting them again and we were pleased to see that their graves had been looked after well and been done up much better than we left. We had a very quiet day otherwise, only with the victory a few of our fellows got a little jubilant, but a couple of hours tied to the wheel of a cart, soon put them right again.[41]

Our next move was into Méteren, where we were fortunate enough to get a nice billet in a roomy loft above an inn.[42] The following morning we got cleaned up and cleaned our guns and ammunition, this we did always on the first opportunity, keeping guns and ammunition always ready for immediate use. After this was over and inspected by the officer we were allowed to do as we liked pretty well, so long as we kept in bounds. During the morning the Commanding Officer read the orders out and I was surprised as well as pleased to hear my name read out for to receive a medal for good work done during the retreat from Mons.

Thursday night saw us off again and this time we got to Bailleul, where we again got

[39] Pte John Copeland from Ballymacarrett, Belfast, was aged 36 when he was killed in action on 26 April 1915. He has no known grave and is commemorated on the Menin Gate at Ypres.

[40] Companies

[41] From the Army Act (renewed annually by Parliament since 1881), the British Army of 1914 produced a Manual of Military Law, rules by which all soldiers knew they had to abide. Commanders had a choice of punishments through which to discipline offenders. Field Punishment Number One was the public humiliation of being tied to a cartwheel for two hours per day, normally for a period of seven days.

[42] Sgt Wilson was often sent in advance to secure billets for his section, and at the same time invariably managed to find very good billets for himself. On this occasion, while the rest of the soldiers were sleeping on pews in a cold church, he was in a warm loft above an inn.

During the First World War, when away from the front-line trenches, the soldiers went to the estaminets or pubs. Here they could buy a hot meal with wine or beer as a welcome respite from the squalor of trench life.

accommodation in a loft. Before our march we saw the French cavalry pass and they looked very smart, although they had been through a bit. All dressed in blue coats with red trousers and wearing their helmets with the hair flowing from them, they looked quite bright towards us. Still I should think they would make a much easier target to hit than we.

Friday the 16th October we continued our march and came upon the outskirts of a large town which we found was Armentières. The enemy were in this town and so we were opened out for to attack. We, with the guns, came through the main street with a few companies in front. As soon as we entered, the Germans left and, but for a few isolated fights in houses and by ways, we went through quite easily. As soon as the inhabitants found out that it was the British who were now in the town they all came out from their cellars and hiding places, and inside a half an hour from being a seemingly deserted town, it was swarming with people, just like walking down Piccadilly.

We halted frequently during our march through and at one place had to remain still for about 3 hours. During this time the people showered us with gifts such as loaves of bread, wine, chocolate, cigarettes etc, also mufflers and gloves. I was lucky to stop outside a large house and was invited in for dinner, so I and the other Sergeant with me went in and had a good dinner he first and I after. The host was a Gendarme or policeman and he was quite excited over the Germans being put out of the town.

There were a few false alarms during this time when shots were fired quite close by, when the people would scatter, shutters up and not a soul in sight, only the military, just in about a minute. They would be out again in a short while though when they saw we were still there.

The order came to push on and so the companies went on and we after them. They looked quite comical as they went by, nearly every man having a great big loaf strapped on the back of his pack. The loaves were round and flat with a hole in the centre, so they were easily carried, and you would see the cavalry men with about 5 or 6 on their arms, having pushed their arms through the holes in the centre. With being white, when they lay down it would be a good aiming mark for the enemy, but so long as they had the bread they did not care for any enemy.

During our stay in the town we did not suffer much from the enemy. A few shells came but went wide of us and we got a few wounded in the house fighting, but they were not wounded in vain for they accounted for a few of the enemy, besides bringing in a few prisoners. When we searched these prisoners it was remarkable to see what they had stored in their pockets. Jewellery, money, sweets, tobacco, soap, razors etc, all mixed up together. The civilians would vain have us given them up to them, one old woman snatching the rifle from one of our chaps and going to shoot them, only he stopped her in time. The people knew what they were, they having been in the town for several days.

As we got to the outskirts of the town we know we were coming in for another little do and so it proved for soon the bullets were heard and our men in front were engaged. They had been gone about an hour when one man coming back wounded told us that Captain Carbery was dead and buried.[43] Quick work but as we were on the move we did not keep the dead long, but buried them at once.

It happened that as our line advanced, they were checked at a farm house. This farm was well protected having walls all round, so the line went on leaving a company to deal with the farm. There was only one entrance and so as our men went in they could not escape. They went in one after the other and every one was killed and they were for still going in only the Captain now in command of the Coy would let no more in. The old Captain having been killed also in trying to make them surrender. There was a good number of Germans in the house so they would not surrender, one man who afterwards got the DC Medal for this act, went in and managed to gain access to the barn beside the house and after liberating some dogs and pigs, set fire to it. It was a very risky thing to do, knowing as he did, that there was seven of our men lying dead inside the door. As he came out he managed to bring the body of the Captain[44] with him and they buried him at once.

Captain Carbery was killed leading his company in the attack on 'Sydney Street' near Houplines.

The line was now several hundred yards in front and so we joined them up, digging our guns in, one on either side of the road. We remained there and at night I had to go back to the limber for some more ammunition and on the way had to pass the farm house. As I passed it was still burning, but had not reached the Germans. One of our Sergeants stopped me and said I must stay and see the fun as the Engineers were putting a charge under the house and were going to blow them all up. So I stayed there in a ditch close by. We got word

[43] Captain Miles Bertie Cunninghame Carbery, 'C' Coy, from Eastbourne was married to the daughter of the late Rt Hon Thomas Sinclair DL of Hopefield House, Belfast. Carbery had joined the Faughs in 1897. He was wounded and taken prisoner during the Boer War and was Adjutant at the Depot in Armagh from 1903 until 1914. He was 37 when he was killed in action. He is buried in Houplines Communal Cemetery Extension.

[44] Captain Carbery

to be ready in case when it blew up any got away. After a few minutes we got the word it was going and then the explosion took place and we couldn't see anything for some time owing to the smoke. Word was then passed for us to double round to the other side of the house and when we got there we saw several who were struggling out of the wreckage, but we soon put them down, all except some who were shouting and had got caught and partly buried. Our officers would not let us go in to see as he said we did not know how many were still in and might play us a dirty trick. As it happened we would not have had much time to go in for just then a regular fusillade broke out and we soon learned that the enemy were attacking and trying to drive us back.

As I had to get ammunition I crept as well as I could back to the limber and had to crawl sometimes where the fire was too hot, under wire fences and the bullets were ringing off the top wires. I eventually got to the wagon and succeeded in getting a few men together and starting back for the guns. The machine guns were firing heavily and here being at the end of the street the lamps were burning so we had to fire at them and put them out. One bullet after going through the lamp went in through the window of a bedroom, and I heard after that the Chaplain was in there, but luckily, it missed him.

The companies who were firing in front now sent back for more ammunition and from being half way back to the guns I turned again and gave them some from our limbers. I got back to the guns but the attack now was slacking off. They were frightened of coming any farther and so they retired again without coming to grips with us. We kept a good fire up after them, for although it was dark and we could not see them, we knew by the firing that they were going back again. This was the first time that I saw the flare used and at first it startled us a bit, to see the whole place lit up like day.'

From midnight until 1.30am on 19 October the enemy lit up the night sky with star shells and machine gunned the line held by the Faughs. The Faughs' defensive trenches were shallow affairs, dug only with entrenching tools[45], in fields to the north and east of Houplines. The Germans attempted to gain some idea of the Faughs' positions by calling out in English for directions. During the day the Faughs were in support of the Seaforths and a little progress was made.

During daylight on 19 October both 'C' and 'D' Companies were in action about Le Ruage, before being relieved that night, except for the Machine Gun Section, which, under Lieutenant Herrick, remained in the line.

The general attack on Frelinghien continued into 20 October, with the Faughs still in position around Le Ruage. The enemy were in trenches to the south of Frelinghien and north of the River Lys. The Seaforths were between the Faughs and the river. Both Regiments attacked together from the left flank using a muddy ditch to make their covert approach. The trenches were eventually taken by a combined charge of the Seaforths and Faughs.

By 9.10am Captain Elkan reported that his company had occupied part of the German trenches; for his skilful leadership before Frelinghien and gallantry at La Ruage he was awarded the DSO.

By 1.30pm 'D' Company held Ferme de la Meularderie on the right and 'A' Company linked 'D' with 'C' on the left. Frelinghien itself was not taken, but the Germans had been driven back into a previously prepared line of trenches.

This trench line established by the Faughs did not move until the closing months of the war.

Back to the journal:

'After things quietened down a bit we lay down to sleep with our sentries posted, but could not sleep with some one in front shouting and groaning and someone in the burning farm behind doing the same thing. We put it down to two Germans and so did not trouble, but when we tried to sleep it became very

[45] Small folding spades carried as part of normal kit, but not much larger than a garden trowel.

annoying and so I said to one of the gunners, a big fellow, that we should creep up to the farm and make him be quiet. As we got near the farm was still on fire inside, and as we got to the window he stopped shouting, so I think he must have heard us. It was amusing though, for as we crept up to the window and just begin to raise our heads to look in, a shot would go off.

As we did not know whether there were any more knocking about inside, we naturally thought they were shooting at us. In the long run we decided to chance it and so crept up over the bricks and fire of one side of the room and the first thing we seen was the German who had been shouting, and no wonder for he was buried amongst bricks up to the neck, not even having his hands out. The smoke was coming out all round so he must have been in a bit of agony, if the fire was at him also. We had our bayonets at his throat but let him off and started to get him out. We got the bricks from him after a bit of hot work as the most of them were red hot. I got him by the arms and started to drag him out, he was only light, but I got a bit of a jump, for I suddenly found two arms hanging down over me and on looking saw it was another German with his helmet on. He was quite safe though for he was dead, having a bullet through his head.

I let the other rest a minute while I looked round this fresh one. He had not got much on him though. It looks bad searching them but we may as well have anything they have as let it be buried with them. I got a few nicknacks off him, but could not get my hand into his trouser pockets as he had stiffened up, the way they do, into a sitting position. There were more lying about dead, but no more living as we could see. We got helmets, rifles and bayonets etc, threw them out to get later for souvenirs. I then dragged this living one out and threw him across my back and carried him out. He was pleased to think we hadn't killed him as he expected I am sure. As he couldn't walk, having his feet burned a little, we took him to our hospital and there it was the first time I had been abused for not killing him. They wanted to know what I had brought him there for, as hadn't they enough to do with our own. When I said I couldn't at the time he said he understood and looked to him. As I was leaving I noticed a gold chain clipped to his pocket, so had it before I left, but it wasn't up to much, one he had taken from some Frenchman as it bore French words on it.

When we got back to the gun again we had some fun, the big fellow who was with me putting on the German's helmet and bending over his chum who was asleep, shook him and told him to surrender. It took him back a little to wake up and find as he thought a big German standing over him. We got no more trouble that night, well I am saying night for now dawn was breaking, so we got what rest we could.

We then crept along with our guns and took up a position in the line with the Battalion. We dug a little trench that day and did not have much to do only bury a few dead Germans. We were all stood up by the trench not thinking of the enemy when suddenly they fired a volley into us but luckily without hitting any one.

The next day at dawn we went back to the road and got into a house where we mounted our guns in the attic, to cover the advance of our men as they were going to push on a bit. It was quite nice watching the attack from here as we could see everything. We could see our shells tearing up the enemies trenches and sending the boards flying, also our men advancing through the fields and we could see they were getting it pretty hot, as the ones they left behind told. At the finish we saw them charge with fixed bayonets and it was good to see the Germans run. The majority of them did not get very far as they were dropped like logs. They got a good number of prisoners also and a good number of them were wounded. When we got to their trenches we found them full of bottles of beer and stuff they had plundered from the village.

We noticed a civilian come from the little village behind and walk towards our lines, but they shot him and it was a pity to see the poor chap rolling about on the ground. He lay still at the finish so he must have died. That civilian and the dead Germans lay out there between the lines for weeks. They were there when we left and may perhaps be there now.

As evening drew near I noticed a number of Germans forming up in front of a white washed cottage and drew my officer's attention to them. He thought they were our own but I said not. They were coming out of the trench and forming up, so I laid the gun on them and judged the distance to be about 600 yards. The officer was looking through his glasses and was now sure they were Germans and said he would let me know when they were all out of the trench. I was getting impatient but at last he said fire and I let hem have a rapid burst and then stopped to hear how they had gone. My officer said a little too high, as when I fired they all looked up at the cottage, so a little turn of the wheel and off I went again. I did not stop this time as I could hear the officer shouting out that I had got them and so I let them have the whole belt and when I had finished I don't think many had got away. The machine gun is a good weapon and we did get our own back occasionally. I should think there would have been about 40 in this batch.

We remained in the house for a few days, having a fairly comfortable time, sleeping on beds but never knowing the minute we would be blown up. Indeed bullets used to come in through the windows as the enemy's snipers knew we were in the house. Each night there was what we used to call a "rattle up" start, that was with it being so dark one side would imagine the others were attacking and so commence firing when the whole line would start. This would be caused by patrols of one side being seen by the other, and so in the darkness they would not know but that the whole lot were moving, and the firing would last an hour or so, before all came quiet again. The nights now began to get a little cold and so we used to look forward to these "rattle ups" for the excitement used to warm us up grand.

Sgt Robert Scott was a close friend of Sgt Hugh Wilson, who described him as a 'proper Irish Paddy'.

I lost another of my chums here named Scott, a proper Irish Paddy, coming from the West of Ireland, and many the good time we had together in peace time.[46] He was shot by a sniper through the head. I remember the day before he was on guard and some German prisoners were brought in, when one of them said something irritating to Scott who promptly gave him a blow with his fist which sent him sprawling about 10 yards away. Poor chap, I remember meeting his wife the night

[46] Sgt Robert Scott from Skreen, Co Sligo, was aged 28 when he died of wounds on 26 October 1914. He is buried at Cité Bonjean Military Cemetery.

before I left Folkestone, for he had only got married and I carried a message to him from her. There was another of our Sergeants got killed now named McEvoy[47] and he was only lately married, and what was more annoying to us was that postcards kept coming from his wife long after he was killed, for two months I should think. Evidently no news of his death had reached her and we were unable to inform her, there being no address on the cards.'

At 7pm on 21 October the enemy made a concerted attack on the Faugh positions using field guns, machine guns and concentrated rifle fire, the whole horrific scene illuminated by star shells. The Faughs repulsed the attack, cheering as the Germans retreated; Brigade HQ sent a message of congratulations to the Battalion. During the night of 23 October the Faughs watched as the church at Frelinghien was burned down in an apparently deliberate act of arson by the Germans.

On 26 October the men of the 10th Brigade came under fire from German trench mortars for the first time, the intention being to drive the Seaforths from their positions in and around the brewery at Frelinghien. The huge bombs fired by these mortars were the size of oil drums and could be plainly seen in flight; falling almost vertically, they demolished whatever they hit. The brewery buildings had provided cover for the German trenches that the Faughs and Seaforths now occupied, leaving them exposed to enfilade fire from their left flank. Lieutenant Penrose was one of several casualties who had to lie until nightfall before they could be evacuated. Only once did the Germans allow four British stretcher-bearers to carry a wounded man to safety in daylight, an act of chivalry so uncommon as to be worthy of record.

During the fighting at Frelinghien the Faughs had the support of one Howitzer[48] under the command of Second Lieutenant A. G. Hess of the Royal Field Artillery. The Faughs were so grateful for the unfailing support of this gun crew that the first share of all comforts acquired by the Battalion were given to the Gunners first. Unfortunately Second Lieutenant Hess[49] was killed a short time later near Ypres. Sgt Wilson desribes these events:

'Wednesday the 21st October, I received my medal[50] from the Commanding Officer, whilst with my gun in the house. I was to have received it before, being warned to be present at some cross roads, where I would have received it in style, but we were under fire at the time and advancing so did not get it then. I was under fire anyhow when he gave it to me in the house. It is a very pretty medal and one the French man thinks a good deal about, being the highest award for gallantry the French soldier can achieve. I packed it up and sent it home, where it arrived safe. The following day was occupied in keeping a watch on the enemy and strengthening our positions.

On Friday we remained in the house on the look out as before, and during these days we were unable to cook anything as the smoke from fires would have given our position away to the enemy's artillery. So I detailed one of our party to go to the limber and get our meals cooked, bringing it back with him. It was a bit risky until he got away over the rise at the back of the house, there being a sniper who could manage to have a view of anyone leaving the garden at the back. I had occasion to go back to the limber during the day and got away all right having to run past a dangerous gap. He fired but was too late. He nearly got me coming back though for he dropped a shot in the ground by my foot, so I did not give him another chance for I ran to the house.

The officer told me when I got back that I

47 Sgt Gordon McEvoy from St Giles, Middlesex, was killed in action on 21 October 1914. He is buried in Houplines Communal Cemetery Extension.

48 A field artillery gun, short and light in proportion to its bore.

49 Second Lieutenant A. G. Hess was killed in action on 24 February 1915.

50 Medaille Militaire

had to get them ready for to move into the trenches as soon as it came dusk. So at dusk we left our house and set off across the fields for the trenches, where we arrived safely. The reason I say safely is because it happened that one may be in the vicinity of the trenches and a rifle fusillade commence or a "rattle up" as we turned in, and then not being near any trench or cover you have to lie down in the open and take your chance. We have had many hit like this, and it feels so miserable lying there not able to do anything while the shots drop all round you, and as the majority know in night firing the shots all go high so that in the trenches you are in comparative safety to those behind. We selected positions for our guns, my gun being on the right and having a good field of fire, that is nothing to obstruct our fire over a large front. We got a place in the line and commenced digging a gun platform and in a few hours we had a fairly good platform and shelter for ourselves made. The position we were in was on the border of a road running across our front, and in front was a ditch and hedge leading down to the road, so that we were content with very little entanglements in front, simply running a few strands of barbed wire through the hedge in front.

The next morning we could observe the Germans' trenches in front, being only a few hundred yards away and it was now we got ourselves into the way of trench warfare, for unlike the trenches about Soissons, we were unable to move about much and dare not show much of ourselves. Sniping now became general all along the line, and our fellows were just as keen watching for the least movement and then firing. News was passed round that the Germans were retreating in front of the Russians, but we did not believe too much, as a great deal of rumours were always about.

Sunday the 25th of October found us well dug in, and lying down all day, listening to very heavy firing on our right. As before, we had to have anything cooked and brought up to us, so that we got hot tea (or was hot when they sent it) at dark and then again at dawn. The cook bringing it to us and taking the things when they were finished back with him. The old chap who was doing cook got used to the safe ways for getting to our trench and at dawn he would wait for the empty dixie until it was getting light, and the longer we were over having it, the more of course he got impatient as it grew light so suddenly. It meant if he stayed too long he would either have to run the gauntlet or stay with us all day in the trench. He found a way out however by bringing it up at 2 or 3 in the morning so we generally were in good form for our next meal at dark.

It was a little misty first thing in the morning, but we could soon see the loop holes of the enemy and amused ourselves by having a pop at them or anything we could see moving, for occasionally we could discern the backs of men and shovels coming up where they were digging. They were very bold these chaps for if we fired at them they would generally wave the shovel to show we had missed, but I don't think we always missed as the shovel sometimes stopped. Our other gun was a little to our left and further back, but they also had a good field of fire and could command the houses in front of them which were occupied with the enemy.

At night we carried planks of wood and doors from a farm house just behind and commenced to make overhead cover to our gun pit. We were working all night and had this done before dawn. This cover above came in very useful, as it kept splinters from shrapnel off us and also to a good extent the rain.

The next day Monday we kept the enemy to our front in his trenches, but to our left they made a strong attack on a village, which was held in certain parts by the Seaforth Highlanders and succeeded in driving the Highlanders slightly back, even when they were a little in advance of our line. The part that annoyed the Highlanders most was having to retire out of a brewery where they had loopholed and had been occupying. One of them said to me they would have fought to the last if they were so allowed, as their officers used to allow them two pints a day. After this affair with the Seaforths, they began to turn their attention to us and we had to stand heavy artillery fire for many hours. The trench being at times full of smoke, and the bursting of the heavy shells about us shook us in our trenches. We lost several killed this day and also about 30 wounded. At night again we were expecting an attack, and so with patrols of both sides going about firing commenced, and for over an hour we had it ding dong, big guns firing also. One shell bursting just above our pit lit the whole place up and nearly made us deaf. We congratulated ourselves on having put up head cover in time.'

By 28 October Battalion HQ was situated in a dugout under Nos 87 and 89 Rue Lutin, Houplines.[51] These numbers must have seemed fortuitous when the frequent enemy shelling destroyed the Chateau just across the road but left the Faughs' dugout untouched. While the Battalion was only playing a secondary part in the current fighting, the men could see and hear the heavy and continuous fighting to the north, and eagerly awaited any news of how it was going. The following day the Germans sent up a captured observation balloon east of Frelinghien. The Faughs could only sit and wait for it, causing a degree of discomfort to them as they feared it would be used to bring down artillery fire.

On 30 October the Battalion war diary records that the Faughs were issued with five loophole plates to protect sentries in the front-line trenches. This was noted as an unusual event because in these early days of the war trench stores were virtually unknown; the soldiers survived by going out during the night and gathering what materials they could find in order to make whatever they needed. The Faughs were obviously on a roll, as the next day they were issued with five Verey flare pistols. It was at this time that the practice of giving soldiers in the front-line trenches a tot of rum was started, after the dawn 'Stand To'. This was thought to be very effective in preventing disease, so was entirely medicinal! The journal continues:

'The next day saw the heavy artillery of both sides at work, the shells passing high above our heads. The houses which we were occupying on this side of the village, were getting a hot time, for the shells that were fired at this part of the village were the heaviest I had heard. They were bursting nearly half a mile off, yet every time they bursted we could feel the earth trembling. Some of our chaps in these houses

Next to the brick house is the empty plot that was the site of Nos 87 and 89 Rue Lutin, Houplines. The Faughs favoured the dugouts under these houses as historically the Regiment began life in 1793 as the 87th and 89th Regiments of Foot.

51 These two houses must have been destroyed at a later stage of the war; the site is still an unused plot.

had narrow escapes. One who was in a room on the ground floor was blown clean through the window on to the road outside and yet never was hurt. It was said that they were using the large guns that they had at Antwerp, but whether this was so or not I could not say. At dark again this day we had another night alarm which lasted about an hour. It was very cold these nights and we welcomed these alarms, for with the excitement we always finished up nice and warm.

On Wednesday we had a fairly quiet day, the man next to me was shot dead. I put a bandage on his head, but he died almost immediately. It seemed strange for just a minute before we were all joking together, and so it was all the time for one never knew the minute he would be shot dead. Apart from all this though we had our bits of sport and I remember seeing a Lance Corporal throwing stones from the trench at some fowls which were scratching just a little in rear. I asked him what he was doing it for and he confessed that during our advance to this trench he had been given the job of burying a dead German.

The bullets were flying about although it was dark and so he and his men dug the grave as quick as possible and you may be sure they did not go too deep. It appears when they put him in it was too small, he being a big man. So they got him in as best they could and covered him up. When the rain came on it partially washed the earth off him and then the hens I suppose thought they could have a go at him. He was throwing stones to chase the hens away for fear the officer found out. So he covered it up better that night and put a board up inscribed "Here lies a German".

Another night we were expecting an attack and so everyone was quiet and listening when suddenly from our trench a hen started screeching. My officer was speaking to me at the time and said "For heavens sake stop that row", but as soon as he spoke it broke out worse then before, and with all being so quiet it seemed to be an awful noise. It was one of the fellows that had collared a rooster from the farm house behind, and was in the act of killing it and getting it ready for the pot. It was a game one for it died lively. If the Germans heard it, they must have envied us.

And so in these trenches we lay day after day, improving them every night and glad when night came to be able to stand up and get out on top for a run. During these days there was nothing but continual sniping and occasionally their artillery would pepper us. They brought down the tree behind our bit and set the haystack on fire, that was just near our trench, so that we were spoiled from getting straw to lie on. They knew this I expect and so set it on fire. We had to keep down that night as the fire lit the whole place up and we could have been easily seen had we moved about.

The nights now were moonlight and we could see across in front fairly clear, and especially with glasses. One night I saw with my glasses whole Battalions behind their trenches. I expect they were getting relieved. Anyhow I reported it but was not allowed to fire as the officer said it was better to keep the gun position secret. It was a pity for we always sight our guns on the trenches before dark, and if we had been allowed to fire we could have scattered them.'

5
November 1914: from Ploegsteert to Messines

On the afternoon of 2 November the Reserve companies of the Seaforths and Faughs were ordered to join the 11th Brigade, near Ploegsteert, known for evermore in the British Army as 'Plugstreet'. 'A' Company, commanded by Major Shuter, marched out of the lines within the hour.

With a full company gone, this was an anxious time for the Faughs. An attack was expected imminently and every man from the Commanding Officer downwards waited in the trenches. There was little hope of reinforcements and they knew they must hold at all costs.

A reassuring message was received from Lord Roberts VC on 6 November: 'Please accept yourself, and convey to your splendid troops, the expression of my highest appreciation of the magnificent gallantry displayed by all ranks, British and Indian.' This was the last message sent by the veteran Field Marshal, who died of pneumonia at General Headquarters, St Omer, on 14 November, aged 82. Born in India of Irish parents, 'Lord Bobs', as he was known to every soldier on the Western Front, had won the Victoria Cross during the Indian Mutiny. He was the last Commander in Chief of the British Army. Sir John Wilson wrote of his death, 'He died as he would have wished himself, in the middle of the soldiers he loved so well and within the sound of guns.'

The attack came on 11 November at 7.30pm and in spite of the strength of the German field guns the Faughs repulsed the attack. The journal recalls:

'The next day Sunday the 1st of November we had a very nice day and the aircraft of both sides took full advantage of it, so that we spent the day in lying down and looking up at the aeroplanes being shelled, and were much interested in a fight between one of ours and one of theirs. They were still at it when they went out of sight so we did not see the finish. One of our aeroplanes was fired on by the whole trenches in front but it still sailed merrily on. This evening at dark we were as usual up on top of the trench having a breather, when all of a sudden we were fired on by a machine gun and it did not take us long to get under, you can guess. They had fired from the top of a house on our left, but luckily no one was hit, although the bullets came almost from the rear. It was moonlight, so they must have seen us.

If you had seen us now in the trenches you would have been surprised, for we had had no wash or shave for a long time and all looked very dirty, our clothes being caked with mud. We had to lie all day and so we all looked eagerly forward to dark when we could stretch ourselves. We heard that the Kaiser was in command of the Army at our front, but could not be sure, anyhow if he was we earnestly hoped one of our long range guns would find his billet. The next day word was passed that the 11th Brigade[52] which was on our left was going to attack and push forward a bit, so we lay listening to this affair and hoping our chaps would succeed, but judging from the fire

[52] See Appendix 4.

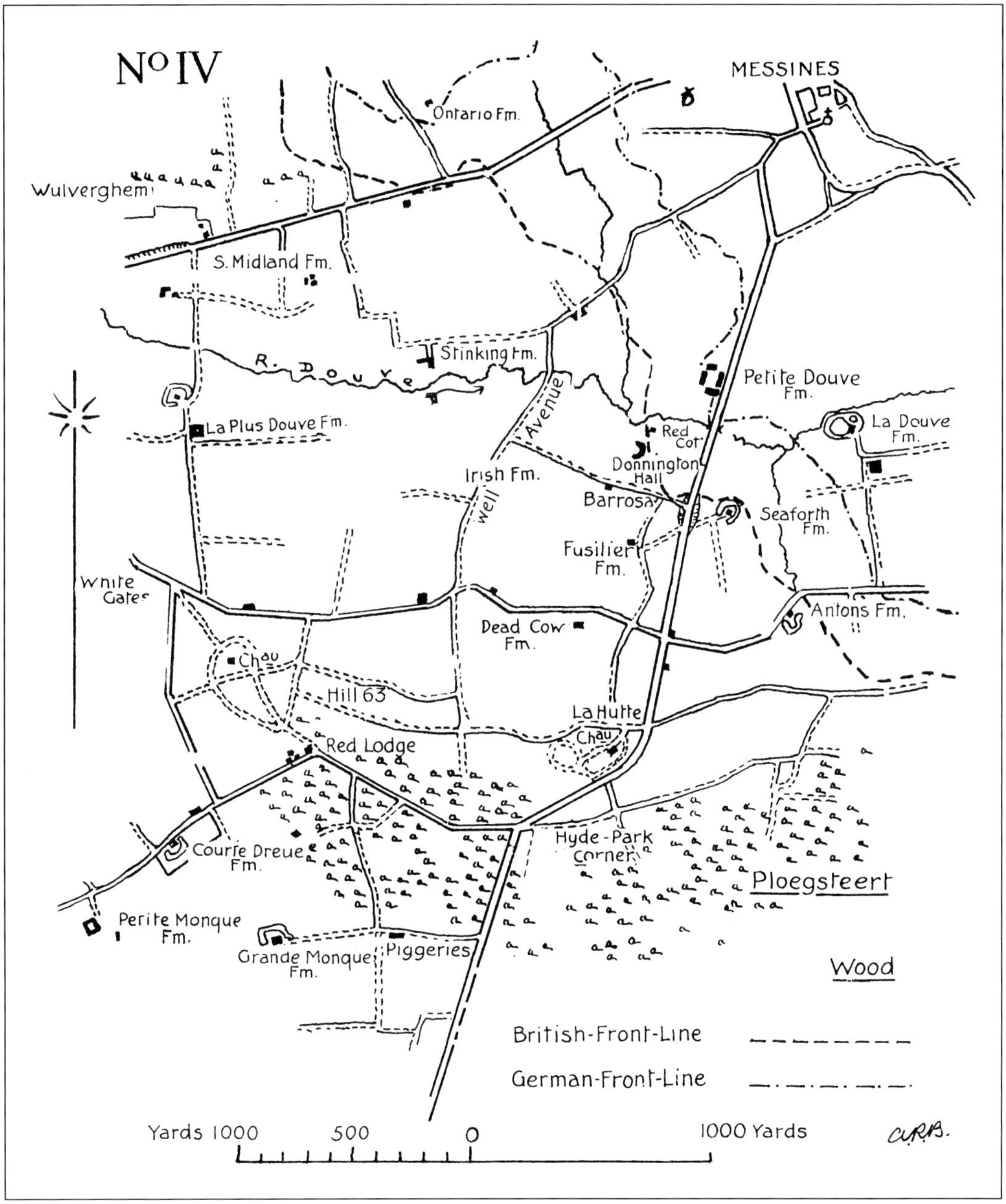

Map showing all the places that became very familiar to the Faughs during the weeks spent in the Douve Sector.

we heard, they must have got it pretty warm. The nights got that bright now it was not safe to get out as we had previously done, for there was a continual fire, what is termed in official notes as "desultory".

The next day was quiet on our front, but heavy cannonading could be heard all day coming from the left. This evening I got relieved by the officer who sent for the other Sergeant and I was glad I can say, if for no

An aeroplane of the Royal Flying Corps.

other reason than to get a wash and brush up. I went down to where the limber was put up just behind some houses, about three quarters of a mile in rear of the trenches. It was quite a change the next day to be able to walk upright in broad daylight and to get washed and cleaned up a bit. I found the men down here had got shelled a good deal as the ground was cut up a good bit by shells, and from one of them I picked up some of the contents, which were very curious being just like cog wheels.

The civil inhabitants still kept to their houses, however, and would only adjourn to a cellar when shelling started. I was billeted with one family and they were always wanting to know whose shells it was that were passing over our heads, and of course, we always said it was ours. When they did know the Germans were shelling they would all run to the one house where there was a big cellar, and when it was finished they would come out. They were all away one time and we were wanting something and could not find anyone. So it suddenly came on me that they were all in the cellar again, so I went to tell them that the shelling was over, and oh they looked such a crew. I am sure there were about 30 in the cellar and one might have thought they were there for days, as they had food etc, spades to dig themselves out, but when I said it was over they would not quite believe it, but eventually came out. I found I had not much to do down here only look after the rations of the men in the trenches, so I took a stroll back to the house of the French man who had been so kind to us previously. He was very pleased to see me and invited me to dinner for which I was grateful as I had not had a civilized dinner for some time. During my stay out of the trenches I slept on the floor in the kitchen of the house, and the floor being tiled, was pretty hard, in fact worse than the trenches as there we had straw.

On Sunday I again visited the house of my friend and after dinner we all went for a walk and visited the Town Hall. This building was almost destroyed by shells, and it was a pity to see the beautiful pictures that were destroyed. As I was coming home again and walking up the street I nearly came in for it again. Along the road, hardly a mile from the trenches, the civilians used to come up on Sundays, just to see how we were doing. This afternoon, however, the enemy must have seen them and let loose a few shells suddenly. I managed to get under cover after the first one, but others were not so fortunate. One child being killed and several soldiers wounded. All this day could be heard a very heavy bombardment to our left.

The French policeman who I had visited wanted me to come again on Tuesday this being Sunday and I promised to, but on Monday I learnt I had to go into the trenches again on Monday night, so decided to go and tell him. When I arrived at his house I found him greatly excited and I learnt that his house had been the victim of one of the enemy's shells. It appeared that early in the morning while he was at work the Germans commenced shelling that part of the town in which his wife and family lived, so they got ready quickly and left the house, leaving a note on the table for him. When he returned at dinner time he found that a shell had come through the bedroom window, smashing the bedrooms up and then finishing off in the kitchen, where they generally lived. It was very lucky for them they had gone in time, although for him, he had to cook his own meals and sleep in the cellar on a mattress. Nevertheless he got a little spread for the two of us and we had a good time. Darkness saw me on my way up to the trenches again and this night was quiet, so I had a good nights rest.

The following day was very cold and our adversaries were quiet, only to the left heavy fighting was going on. The sound of the guns firing was very clear, especially the French guns which we could tell by the double report. The next day was as the previous one, heavy firing on the left, and nothing doing to our front, only the usual sniping. At night we had an alarm which lasted for an hour. We were shelled at the same time, so it was quite lively while it lasted, but not doing much damage as only a few men were wounded. The next day was very cold and we lay all day on our straw beds and when night came we improved our trench again making our head cover a little stronger.

The enemy at this time took to shelling the town of Armentières which lay behind us and did much damage to the houses and civil population. The next day the artillery on both sides were at it as usual. This day while in the trench I received the Conspicuous Conduct card[53] from Major General Wilson, who was in command of our Division. The next day was

Lt Barefoot in a straw-lined shelter or dug-out at Frelinghien in November 1914.

[53] This was in recognition of Sgt Wilson's bravery during the Battle of Le Cateau.

quiet except for sniping. One man close by was killed by a bullet coming through the loop-holes. At night I got relieved again and was very glad as I enjoyed the previous rest I had. On our gun team we had enough men to leave a few behind and so relieve each other occasionally.'

Major Shuter and 'A' Company rejoined the battalion on 14 November, having had an exciting time fighting the Germans in and around Ploegsteert Wood. By mid-November the weather had turned both wet and cold with severe frosts at night, but despite the appalling weather conditions morale remained high. Of the original 23 Battalion officers, only 14 now remained, the rest having been killed or wounded. Since Cromwell's time British Army officers have led their men into battle from the front. On the Western Front in 1914, the white embroidered badges of rank on the lower sleeves of officers' tunics made them especially easy targets.

The Royal Welch Fusiliers and the Scottish Rifles relieved the Battalion on 17 November, so the Faughs gladly packed up their gear and meagre belongings and marched to new billets on farms south of Ploegsteert for a few hours deserved rest and some hot food.

The following day the Faughs relieved a battalion of the Royal Scots in what was known as the Douve Sector. The Battalion marched by companies from their billets, heavily weighed down, for all rations, ammunition and trench stores had to be carried by hand. The route lay to a fork in the road south of Hill 63, known as Hyde Park Corner, thence to Red Lodge, and from there in single file through the chateau grounds, by White Gates to La Plus Douve Farm. From there it was an ice-covered muddy tramp to the trenches. While this was a wide detour to get into position, it was necessary as the main Messines Road was swept by enemy fire. Alternating with their friends the Seaforths, the Faughs held this sector for the next five months. Sgt Wilson takes up the story:

'The next day, Sunday the 15th November, I was enjoying a rest in the same billet as previously and in the afternoon went down to see my chum the French man. I stayed indoors most of the time as it was very wet and windy, so that the shelling was knocked off a good bit.

On Monday the enemy gave the town behind a severe shelling and made an awful mess of the place. I was out at dark and the shells were passing over the streets with an awful screech, that sounded worse with it being quiet and dark. They were trying to knock a bridge down but did not succeed in hitting it, instead they dropped several into the houses on either side and in one case killed a whole family who were seated round a table. One of our chaps who saw it, said it was an awful sight. Word now came that we were to hold ourselves in readiness to move off at any moment, to where not known. We did no more this day, but the next evening saw us on the road once more. As far as we know we were going to some rest camp and then on again into the thick of it. But as events proved we were going straight into the thick of it.

When we had been in these trenches one of our Companies, along with one Coy of each of the other Battalions in our Brigade had gone away and been away a week at a place called Ploegsteert. They had had a bad time of it, for they lost 60 killed and wounded inside a week. They were back however now and were telling us that this was the way they had gone, that we all were going now, so we were looking forward to having a good time as well as a warm one.

The trenches we left were taken over by another Brigade and they were well pleased with the condition they were in, and no doubt they were good as our men had been constantly at work on them. It was about 10 pm when we left and after marching about 3 hours we arrived near the village of Ploegsteert in which we were lucky to find good billets in a house that was empty but had beds etc, so we were very comfortable. We could hear rifle fire going on quite close, but for all that we enjoyed a good nights rest, I with a Corporal sharing a good bed. The following day we did nothing but clean up and were looking forward to another night in bed, but we lost that, for orders came at dusk to move, and this time we marched on until we came very close to the enemy as we could tell by the silence we had to keep.

It was a long march this and the snow commenced to fall so that we were very miserable. As we got near the trenches we could see that heavy fighting had been taking place and each Company was told off to their positions and went off independently. We went off on our own also, having a guide with us as did the Companies. We were packed up like mules with guns, ammunition etc. and had to move very slowly in single file as the ground would not be seen with the snow. It was a miserable do this, for it seemed so long and none of us knew where we were going.

I remember passing some of our guns, and we would not have known there were any guns there only for the sentry's challenge. He said as we passed him, that the old chateau, standing above on the hill, was empty and the cellars were all full of nice food and bottles of wine in abundance. So we felt sorry we could not stay. After a lot of halting and resting, for we had to rest frequently, being different to the Companies as we had so much weight to carry, we arrived at the trenches. They were not trenches, being just a few spade fulls of earth shovelled out and not waist deep, and besides being half full of water. So one can judge our feeling after marching so far to arrive in a place like this. The enemy were just a little in front, so we had to keep down, but the majority, before standing up in water sat up on the bank, and took their chances of being hit. We got our guns mounted as best we could for our hands were nearly frozen and so was the water in the guns I am sure, so if we had to fire I am afraid we would have been in a fix, still we always carried our rifles and bayonets, that is all except the two men who fire the guns.

There was a few houses about and a good number of farms. One house just by where we were had not been touched by fire as yet, so I took a stroll round and went in and found the kitchen full of our fellows, all crowded round a little fire, trying to warm themselves. You could not blame them and I asked what they were doing in there instead of in front in the trench. They said they would fly out at the first shot. They would have done too, of course, so I had not the heart to turn them out. The sentries of course were in the trench, poor chaps with their feet frozen.'

The Faughs' position rested on the road at Anton's Farm, where it linked up with the sector held by the Royal Dublin Fusiliers and Royal Warwickshire Regiment. It then ran north-west across ploughed fields to the moated farm subsequently known as Seaforth Farm[54]. From here it turned west across the Messines Road and, taking in Donnington Hall and Red Cottage, ran north to the River Douve, which was the dividing line between divisions. In total, it was a trench line of 1,200 yards (see the map on page 70).

A combination of heavy rain and the flooding of the Douve had turned the Flanders clay into glutinous mud. The trenches had previously been hurriedly dug by the French and now had to be deepened and also adapted to cope with the mud. Thus, according to the 1st Battalion war diary, the Faughs invented what became known as 'duck-boards'. The wood was cut from the copses that lay behind the line, and the boards' primary use was to enable the men to lie down, which was otherwise impossible. At the end of the war there were thousands of miles of trenches laid with 'duck-board' tracks, and few if any trees!

The position was dominated by the Messines Ridge. From the church and buildings of Messines village, the Germans had a bird's eye view of the British trenches and could accurately target their artillery fire. The British artillery was positioned on and south of Hill 63.

[54] Just to the north of this farm the Irish Peace Tower now stands dominating the Messines Ridge. It is reminiscent of an Irish round tower and was built by young people from both traditions and from both sides of the Irish border. It was jointly opened by HM Queen Elizabeth II and the Irish President Mary McAleese in 1998.

Battalion Headquarters was first located in a dugout west of Irish Farm, but was frequently moved to different points in the support trenches, including Red Lodge and finally Barrosa Farm[55]. The most memorable dugout was a small cellar under Seaforth Farm, measuring 12 feet by 6 feet; although below the level of the moat, frequent bailing kept it fairly dry. It was completely unapproachable during daylight, but with a small brazier in the corner it offered a warm welcome to the Battalion officers at night.

Sgt Wilson describes conditions in the trenches:

> 'The next day at dawn we had to keep low, not knowing exactly how far or near the enemy were. We had managed to get a little straw during the night, but soon the water came through and to make matters worse the snow kept on. So one can imagine what sort of day we passed, crouched down on wet straw with our feet and hands like ice and the snow giving us a counterpane to cover us. The Regiment who were in these trenches before we came in had only got there the night before having had some hard fighting to get that length, so they had not had time to dig themselves in.
>
> We found that the enemy were very close, as when we were lying down we heard several shots pass just over our heads, and learnt that three of our fellows were wanting to get across to another part of the trench and had got up and ran across. They did not get very far before two were killed and the other wounded, he ran on and managed to get in. We always found that until we got used to our new surrounding, every time we moved, that we lost many men. Getting to know the dangerous corners so to speak. There was hardly a night passed but we had a burying party out. During the whole of this day we had nothing to eat or drink and with the cold and wet I think it was the most miserable day I ever spent, but one soon forgot it. As dark came on we managed to make some tea in a little mud hut, but had to be very careful not to make any sparks with the fire, as the least movement or light drew the enemy's fire.
>
> The snow being on the ground it was quite easy for us to see figures of the enemy moving about, and of course we could be seen quite as easily, at least we thought so by the bullets that kept singing round us. During the night we were employed improving the trench and next morning we were under cover from gun fire a little better. At dawn this morning we lost one of our officers who was shot through the head and later in the day several men were killed and wounded.
>
> The next day we were still in misery with the cold and wet, for as yet we had no proper dugouts made to shelter us. Word came this day that we were getting relieved at night by the Seaforths and so it need not be said that we were all pleased. At night the Seaforths came up and took over our positions, and they were not well pleased at the prospects of serving in such trenches. For us it was quite a relief to get out of fire and be able to walk upright again.'

On 19 November Brigadier General Hull took over command of the 10th Brigade from the newly promoted Major General Haldane. The first leave was granted to officers, one per battalion, and Captain Bull was the lucky man in the Faughs. There was also an issue of winter clothing, goatskin coats and mackintosh capes. Both were most welcome, as the regulation greatcoat was totally unsuitable for the trenches; a wet and muddy greatcoat could add an extra 50lb or 23kg to a man's weight.

The remainder of the month was spent settling down into trench routine. Every four days the Seaforths and Faughs exchanged places and soon every officer and man knew the line so well that, even on the blackest of nights, the reliefs were carried out swiftly and with little incident. Moving in and out of the trenches was always a very

[55] It was at Barrosa near Cadiz that the 87th Foot (later the 1st Battalion Royal Irish Fusiliers) was the first regiment in the British Army to capture one of Napoleon's Imperial Eagles during the Peninsular War.

dangerous activity. If the Germans spotted the slightest sign of movement, flares were sent into the air, swiftly followed by machine gun and artillery fire.

Behind the lines the battalions were billeted in Armentières and Nieppe. In the latter the Faughs enjoyed hot food and a hot bath in the Brasserie Esperance, where large beer barrels had been cut in half to make bathtubs! Sgt Wilson continues:

> 'We marched about 5 miles into Nieppe, a fair sized town. We knew this town, as previously we had driven the Germans from it. The walk did us good and although the roads were in a bad mess and the night cold, we felt the blood beginning to circulate again and ourselves warming up, so that by the time we got to our quarters we felt ourselves once more. For anyone to have seen us in daylight I am afraid we looked awful sights, with the mud plastered all over us. Anyhow the next day we all got a hot bath and a change of linen, so after that and an hour or so cleaning the mud off ourselves, we were quite fit again.
>
> We, the machine gun detachment, found ourselves billeted in a brewery, and found it not too bad, having plenty of straw to lie on. It was very nice to be able to walk about the streets with our heads up and not to hear the continual sounds of gun and rifle fire. However we were not allowed to remain long here, for on the second day we got notice to go into the reserve trenches, and were lucky enough to get billeted in a farm house behind the hill which was between us and the enemy. We were sheltered from view here, but that did not prevent us from an occasional shell, a few shells having hit the house, but not doing very much damage. We on the machine gun got a little kitchen at the back of the house, which was very useful as besides cooking we were able to dry our ammunition belts which were always wet after leaving the trenches. There was a moat around this house which was full of gold fish and the grounds were very nice, and in the fields close by were vegetables, so we had vegetables for a change. On the back of this kitchen was a little room in which there was a bed, so I and a Cpl shared it, so that although we were in sound of the fire we were very comfortable.'

The farms south of Hill 63 also offered good billets. Here the best was the 'Piggeries', where the all brick pigsties, once thoroughly cleaned, provided good cover and warm, dry quarters for the men. Not that they spent much time there. When out of the trenches the men spent their days drilling, training, exercising and cleaning their equipment. At night the soldiers were sent on working parties, bringing rations and ammunition up the line or improving and repairing the trenches. A combination of enemy shellfire, the rain, thawing snow and floods caused a lot of damage to the trenches, so every scrap of wood was scavenged and used to shore up the trench walls.

It was at this time that the British artillery ran short of ammunition, and the enemy artillery could not be engaged in counter battery fire. The Germans were quick to catch on to this and began to bring their guns up close to the British position to engage in direct fire. The result of this was deeper and narrower trenches, which, although they could still be seen, were harder to hit.

Perceptibly small comforts began to appear: braziers, together with a supply of coke and coal, and small hand carts fitted with old motor-car tyres, which made the transport of supplies easier. The officers of the Battalion purchased a local farm cart, which the Mess Sergeant converted into a portable field kitchen; the carts later became part of the Regimental transport and were issued by the Ordnance Department. Gumboots were also issued to the officers and men for the first time, though they were only useful where the mud or water in the trenches was not too deep. Sgt Wilson describes the conditions:

> 'The next day was cold but nice and clear so we had a football match to while away the time and to warm us up. The next day we were still in the same position and were for the trenches at night to relieve the Seaforths. It commenced to rain so that the snow disappeared and left as usual mud. At dusk we

Above The 'Piggeries' in Ploegsteert, south of Hill 63. Here the Faughs stage a fake photograph of the execution of a 'spy', who in reality is Pte Bailey, the Officers' Mess Cook. Presumably he was not a very good cook!

Below The 'Piggeries' in Ploegsteert in 2004.

started on our way to the trenches and we could not get the limber too close. It had to be left at the gates of a lodge and I was lucky to be left in charge of it. After the team had left and I had seen all the carts covered up I went into the lodge and along with another Sgt got a good bed. He was left to look after rations. All these houses we came to had been deserted and everything had been left just as it was, so that there were plenty of beds, pots, pans and even the canary we had to look after.

The next day was quiet where we were, but we could hear the heavy shells bursting about the trenches, so thought ourselves lucky to be here. During the day I did a bit of exploring and went up the hill in front and got a good view of the country in front, being able to see the trenches of both sides quite plain. Of course I had to keep as low as possible, for once over the hill in front, one was quite easily seen. I visited the old chateau and found that during our absence it had been bombarded and set on fire. It had a lovely tower, so that from the top one could see for miles, so that was the reason the enemy destroyed it. They had not destroyed it completely for the ground floor and cellars were intact. It must have been a lovely place as the marble and bronze statues which were all over the place, and the great clocks and other beautiful things lying about testified. There were plenty of nice plates and glasses etc and I got a few for our own use at the lodge. The Germans of course had had the first helping as the belongings of them were left here and there.'

To the men in the ranks came a supply of gifts and food, courtesy of Mrs Douglas Churcher, wife of the late Commanding Officer, and Mr Delmege Trimble, editor of the *Armagh Guardian*. Between them, for the duration of the war, they provided not only for the men in the trenches, but also for those Faughs who had been taken prisoner. While the Battalion lost only a few men as POWs (mostly those wounded and worn out on the long retreat from Mons), all were thankful for the food that allowed them to survive their time in German prison camps. In 1920, while the Battalion was serving in Persia, it sent three fine Persian carpets to Mr Trimble as a way of saying thanks.

In 1915 Lady Dartrey organised the collection of £1,314 from all denominations in the counties of Armagh, Monaghan and Cavan, and was able to send three motor ambulances to France for use by the Battalion. She also endowed a bed in the UVF Hospital in Belfast, which was home to numerous wounded soldiers for many years after the war ended. Two of the inscribed brass plates from the ambulances were brought home by men of the 36th Ulster Division and presented to Lady Dartrey. The third ambulance was believed to have been destroyed by shellfire.

On 23 November Father Ryan[56] joined as Chaplain to the Battalion and proved popular with the men. Captain R. W. R. Jeudwine also joined, bringing with him a draft of 103 replacements. The Captain was most annoyed to lose his brand new hat to an enemy shell within minutes of arriving in the trenches. For the remainder of the month the Battalion suffered near constant shellfire, and Second Lieutenant Cooke was wounded on the 29th. Towards the end of the month Warrant Officers and non-commissioned officers were allowed to go on ten days' furlough; the first to go were Regimental Sergeant Major Scrafield and Regimental Quartermaster-Sergeant Robinson.

The jounal continues:

'The following day the snow had all gone and in the morning I had another walk round. We

[56] 4024 Pte John Coogan from St Patrick's Terrace, Armagh, mentioned Father Ryan in one of his letters home to his mother on 21 April 1915: 'Today, Sunday, Father Ryan said Mass for us in the little village [Merris] chapel where we are billeted. It was a surprise for us to see him amongst us again, and everyone was delighted to see him again. I don't know whether he is going to stop with us for good. I hope he will for he is a very nice jolly man.' Pte Coogan was aged 24 when he was killed in action on 25 April 1915. He has no known grave and is commemorated on the Menin Gate at Ypres.

Right **Father G. Ryan CF, one of five Roman Catholic priests who ministered to the 1st Battalion Royal Irish Fusiliers during the Great War, indicative of the fact that the predominant religion of the men of the 1st Battalion was Roman Catholic.**

had to be constantly on the alert for aeroplanes of the enemy, for if they spotted us we knew what to expect. Someone must have been seen, for that evening we got a gentle reminder as suddenly the shells came from over the rise in front. A few burst just on the hill in front and the bullets came whistling down amongst us. I was standing in the room of the lodge, facing the hill, and a bullet from one of the shells came through the window, passing behind my head and burying itself in a picture on the wall. Another piece knocked a pane of glass out, so I thought it was time to move and so I went down to the back of the house where there were already a good number. The big shells now came at intervals and we could hear them coming and it seemed that each one would knock the top of the house off. They just scraped over and dropped in the field behind,

Below **One side of the Ypres (Menin Gate) Memorial, which commemorates those killed near Ypres and who have no known grave.**

not doing much damage only to the ground and hitting us with a lump of mud now and again. It was quite exciting while it lasted, every shell as it would be heard coming would see us all away into the side of the house and when it passed, out again we came.

The next day I and another Sgt went for a walk into the village of Ploegsteert for a little exercise. It was a nice day so we enjoyed it, and were able to buy bread and milk in the village. The enemy thought it worth while to drop a few shells round the church while we were there and as it looked as if he was going to keep the game up we thought it wise to depart, for we had our share the previous night. The road was a good one only it was covered with holes made by shells which were very dangerous, especially at night when transport was moving along them. It was all wood round here and there had been some hard fighting as we could see by the trenches full of water and bits of dugouts with rifles broken, bayonets and bits of equipment, mostly French, for they had been there previously. We could hear the trenches in front getting heavily shelled and learned at night that we had lost several, killed and wounded.

The next day Sunday, was our turn out of the trenches and we heard we were going to Pont de Nieppe again, so were pleased, and only hoped we might get staying there a little longer. Having another Sgt now on the gun detachment I was able during the last four days to have a relief, along with a few of my men, who would the next time we were for the trenches go in and others stay out. This was the only way we could work reliefs, the Companies were a little better, being able to leave a Company out during the day, in the reserve trenches. At dark when the horses came up I got all ready and moved off with the limbers up the road to meet the team coming out of the trenches. I was pleased to learn that they had not suffered any casualties, the Coys had not been so fortunate however.

We marched into Nieppe and were billeted in a brewery once again, but got no bath this time although we could have done with one. We spent two days here and the second day we got some new parts to our guns and so left to try them, but when we got to the place I found out we were not allowed to fire there, so had to postpone it for some future time. During our stay here I met my cousin who was in the same Regiment. It is surprising, that although he had come out with the Battalion at the start, how little we had seen of one another.'

6
December 1914: the Christmas and New Year truces

In December His Majesty King George V toured France inspecting the various units of the British Expeditionary Force, and at Nieppe on 2 December he presented decorations and gallantry medals to several soldiers. During the ceremony Lieutenant J. C. O'Brien led the platoon of the Faughs that took part in the parade, and several medals were awarded to the Faughs for gallantry during the attack at Houplines. Captain R. J. Kentish received the Distinguished Service Order[57] and Privates Barton and Leddy the Distinguished Conduct Medal.

The winter weather left the trenches in an appalling state. They could only be kept clear of water by the use of pumps constructed by the Royal Engineers using corrugated iron. On 5 December Captain (and Adjutant) W. H. C. Wortham was admitted to hospital; he had been unwell for some time, but had remained on duty until he was physically unable to carry on. Captain P. Penn took over the duties of Adjutant.

Added to the near constant bombardment from enemy guns was the ever-present danger from snipers. In this the Faughs could hold their own: with no shortage of small arms ammunition, a steady fire was directed towards the enemy lines. While casualties from sniping were not severe, good men were lost. On one particularly pitch-black night Company Sergeant Major Sproule[58] was shot dead.

The trench periscope was invented to protect against snipers, and the Battalion tested it in December. The early versions were very basic, made from cardboard and mirrors, but proved effective in enabling the soldiers to watch the enemy without putting their heads above the parapet. Sgt Wilson records in his journal:

> 'Tuesday, the 1st of December we left at 4.30 pm for the same billet as previously and were successful in getting established in the same kitchen as before. The next day we paraded and marched into Nieppe to try our guns, hoping to get firing this time. We arrived at Nieppe and were pointed out the place where some one had been firing previously and proved our guns satisfactory for any German, too good they were for the shots penetrated the target and went through the wall into the back of some man's garden. On the way back we were held up on the bridge on account of the King's visit, and so we formed up and when he came gave him the "present arms". He was accompanied by the Prince of Wales and they both looked well. They inspected our bathroom in the brewery. During their visit the King presented some DC medals and one of ours got one. Pte Leddy who was in the farm house outside Armentières previously mentioned. He had three now, having got the

[57] While HM the King pinned the decoration to his tunic, HRH the Prince of Wales handed Captain Kentish the case and ribbon of the order, after which both shook hands with him.

[58] CSM Joseph Sproule from Kesh, Co Fermanagh, was aged 31 when he was killed. He has no known grave and is commemorated on the Ploegsteert Memorial.

two South African medals. He was a good sort and I was sorry to hear later that he had been killed at Ypres.

We returned to our billet and the following day at dusk went up to the trenches. This day had been quiet, but to the left, Ypres direction, a heavy fire by our guns had been kept up all day. We arrived at the trenches safe, but went through a good deal of sniping as it was a clear moonlight night and our forms could be seen by the snipers. We took over our usual positions which were a little better now, as all night long was spent by working parties improving them, they were damp and wet through, but we could always get dry straw from a haystack behind, which kept for a night, the next morning it would be wet through. The usual sniping went on and an occasional man of ours would go down. I moved with my gun team to another part of the line, where we made a good gun pit and had a grand field of fire, being able to sweep the ground from right to left from the enemy's trenches to our own.

This night and the next day it rained all the time, with an occasional hail storm, so that the trenches got into an awful state, being ankle deep and in some places knee deep with water. Our dugout were the same, the straw floating about inside, so that it was a case of standing up the whole time. We got buckets and old cans to keep bailing out, but it came back again and did not seem to get any less. The artillery had a duel overhead, but the infantry in front were quiet like ourselves, and we could see them throwing the water out of their trenches also, so a sort of sympathy existing between us, very little firing was done that day. At night though the firing commenced again, and we lost a Sergeant of ours, who was shot through the neck.[59] The cold was severe also, so that we were very miserable, and it was not uncommon to catch the sentries standing on top of the parapet, hoping to get shot they felt that miserable. My sentry and I caught up in this position and he was saying to himself as the bullets sang past him "For God's sake hit me". I told him to come down and not be a fool, as it would not last for always. The only thought I had, was that it would be awful to die in such filth and mud and have to be buried in slutch[60].

The following day was Sunday and was a little better not being so cold and the rain having ceased, and we occupied our time in digging where the walls had fallen in. This was dirty work as in places it was feet deep in water and mud. The artillery were at it as usual and sniping was kept up so that we had to keep our heads low while working. My cousin had been slightly wounded a little before this, and was now back again in the trenches. His Company being next to me I could see him now when ever I wished.'

In December a new system of relieving troops was introduced. The usual four days in the trenches, then four days on working and carrying parties was followed by a further four days well to the rear. This meant that the Faughs could spend four days in the village of La Crèche, where the men could be well rested. The first day in the village was spent in washing, the second in ceremonial drill, which seemed to be liked by the men. Later there was sometimes the chance to go into Nieppe and visit the 'Follies', a troupe of amateur entertainers created by the staff of the 4th Division.

The journal goes on:

'The next day it commenced to rain again, but this did not prevent the artillery having their customary display on our trenches. With the rain, we have constantly to be bailing out, and digging the way clear, as the banks keep falling in. At night a heavy rifle fire commenced, and we thought we would be unable to get relieved

[59] 7917 Company Sergeant Major Joseph Sproule was born in Kesh, County Fermanagh, and was killed in action on 8 December 1914 at Douve. He has no known grave and is commemorated at the Ploegsteert Memorial.

[60] A term used by canal workers from the North of England to mean dredged-up mud or silt.

this night, as it was our turn to go out. We, doing four days in and four out at the time. At last the fire ceased and the Seaforths came up and relieved us, and glad we were for it had not been a pleasant time for us and we were one cake of mud. This time we were to become Divisional Reserve[61] and marched to a village about five miles behind the lines, arriving about one o'clock the following morning. The Companies were distributed about in farms and we got a nice little barn for a billet, which just held us comfortably. This was just a small village and near an important railway junction, but one thing it was quite a nerve relief being out of sound of the continual gun and rifle fire. We spent the two days we were here in getting the mud off ourselves and cleaning our guns.

We again went into Brigade Reserve and marched to the farm in which we were before and got the same kitchen to stay in. In the evening we could hear heavy firing close by on the night and got the order to stand to, but after some time we were dismissed, the Companies coming back again, the attack had failed. The following day the Battalion moved up to the trenches again. I stayed at Lodge, it being my turn out this time.'

Lt Le Mare in waders and leather jacket in the waterlogged trenches of the Douve sector during the winter months of early 1915.

On 10 December news was received of the British naval victory in the Falkland Islands. In mid-December some Faughs were transferred to the newly formed Divisional machine gun batteries. To confuse the German snipers and prevent them from targeting officers too easily, all officers began to wear the same webbing as the men. Also, the marks of rank were changed from white embroidery to darkened metal and worn on the shoulders instead of the cuffs. It was eventually realised that officers' swords were no longer of any practical use, and they were ordered to send them home.

Consequences of the cold, wet weather were that men had to stand for hours at a time up to their knees in waterlogged trenches. Frostbite, trench foot and trench fever became a problem for all troops. It could take a soldier several weeks to recover from these illnesses, which had obvious implications for manpower levels in the front-line trenches. To try and prevent frostbite the soldiers were issued with mineral or petroleum jelly to massage into their limbs and boost blood circulation. Trench foot was caused by long periods of immersion, resulting in badly swollen, blistered

[61] Soldiers were moved as a Brigade or Division into Reserve to give them a chance to rest, recuperate and recover from the constant shelling and fear of death. The Reserve areas, often encampments at this stage in the war, were usually well behind the front-line trenches and out of range of enemy artillery.

flesh. If untreated the flesh would become numb, then black and eventually gangrenous. It was thought that whale oil would make the feet waterproof, so soldiers were made to rub it into their skin. It must have added another layer of stench to the trenches. To prevent the condition becoming serious the soldiers' feet were inspected every day by a Senior NCO or a subaltern.

Trench fever was a more severe problem. This was a type of typhus caused by the infected bite of body lice, in which every soldier was covered. It was also highly infectious and outbreaks quickly reached epidemic proportions. The main cause of death was a high temperature that could last for two weeks, leading to heart failure. Thankfully the Battalion suffered little with this ailment.

Body lice were a real problem for the soldiers in the trenches. It was a normal sight to find the men stripped to the waist, killing the lice that hid in the seams of their clothes.

The effectiveness of the Maxim machine gun as a weapon of mass destruction was now accepted by the War Department and the allocation to all regiments was increased. In December the Faughs received another two machine guns, bringing the Battalion total to four. By contrast, a German battalion had six, and from August 1915 that would be increased to 12.

On 20 December the Battalion provided fire support in an attack made by the 11th Brigade on the right flank. The Germans were quick to retaliate and for the next two days the Faughs' positions were bombarded by very accurate fire. Luckily their trenches were very deep so casualties were kept to a minimum. Little could be done except watch the missiles fly over, and repair the damaged trenches by night. The journal takes up the story:

> 'The following days it was fairly quiet, only for the usual sniping and an occasional burst of fire by the artillery. We received our letters regular now, it taking about three days. Plenty of comforts commenced to come out now, and we were well supplied with mufflers, socks etc. Word came that the French were going to attack on our left and the artillery was told off to keep the enemy engaged to our front. They were concentrated for this and the fire they poured on the enemy was terrific, nothing could be heard but a continuous roar of guns. Their artillery replied feebly, dropping a few close by but doing no damage. The house I was in swayed with this bombardment, so that I thought the best place was outside in case any of it came loose. The following day was very dull, but the artillery kept up fire until dark. My cousin was slightly wounded this day and went into hospital. I saw him off and he was quite cheerful, saying he would be back again soon.
>
> The fourth day we left for the village five miles away and remained there two days after which we came to the farm by the firing line as before. While out of the trenches, everything was done for us that could be, boots supplied, underwear, and comforts of every kind. We got issued with skin jackets which were very warm, but once they got wet,

it took days to dry them. Waterproof coats were given out which proved very useful, as they had no sleeves in, but a cape attached and these were worn on all occasions in the trench. During the evenings whilst at rest, we would organise concerts and used to have plenty of fun. Later on we could go by bus to a theatre in a large town close by, and by paying 6d[62] enjoy a good entertainment. The chief feature of one was two French girls trying to sing Tipperary in English, but they were good as a rule.

We on the gun team, used to sit in the evenings round our fire in the little kitchen of the farm, and many a good hour we spent singing and telling yarns. During the day we had football matches, and the excitement was keen, for one never thought much that some of those playing or watching were doing so for the last time, as there was not a time we went up to the trenches, but we lost someone.

We got the same rations out of the trenches as in, but while out we could cook them better, and have a little extra at times, for we always could get eggs from the farms and milk also. In the trenches we had to cook as best we could and were only allowed to light a fire at dark and dawn and do our cooking then. At dawn it was quite comical to see the whole lines, both ours and the enemy's with smoke coming out, looking as if it was coming out of the earth. They evidently had the same orders as ourselves. As day light came the smoke would disappear and then looking towards the enemy's lines we could see his cemetery just above us on the hill.

Our guns and rifles were doing their work, as we could notice the crosses getting more numerous, as indeed our own were, as we had a carefully kept little grave yard just behind the trenches. When we came to this position, the fighting had not become settled like it is now, so that when men were killed they were for the most part buried where they fell, and it is common to see graves all about the trenches, sometimes just at the parapets. At one dugout I was in there was a German buried not two yards away, and this was the third resting place he had had, the first time he was dug up by a working party in the trench, they buried him afresh but a shell dislodged him again and now he is within a foot or so of my dugout. In the next dugout I came to there was one of our own men buried just up on the bank, so that I had to tell men that came there not to be throwing tins up there as one of our chaps was buried there.

Saturday the 19th of December was our turn for the trench again. I saw the teams off, of which we had four all under a NCO and going to different positions along the line. I stayed down at the time, but had to go up later at night. Accordingly, when it came time for to go I set off, taking a short cut I had marked out previously. However, I was destined to have a most exciting night, for the night being rather misty and no moon out, I wandered off my path. I had no rifle with me, but was carrying my blanket and oil sheet, having my great coat on with my equipment on the top as was the custom. The first indication that I had strayed from my correct course was when I had been walking about half an hour, I did not seem to be any nearer, when in that time I should really have been there. I made for some trees in the distance which I thought were near to the trench, but when I arrived I found I could get no further as they were all enclosed in barbed wire. I then walked along to the left as I thought it would be the right direction, and after walking some time and tumbling in some disused trenches which were half full of water.

I arrived up against more barbed wire. The best thing left I thought would be to go back from where I had come and start again, and while I was standing considering, a shot sang past and buried itself in the ground a few feet away. I then made off to go back, and as I turned another bullet went past my ear, so

[62] Six old pence (the d stands for denarius, the ancient Roman silver coin).

The unsophisticated British barbed wire fences of the early months of the war.

wherever I was I was seen and I therefore got out of the way as quick as I could. I afterwards found out I was trying to get through the enemy's barbed wire. It was a good job I did not succeed. After walking for a good while I began to think I was near to where I started, when suddenly a regular fusillade broke out along the whole line and the bullets were dropping all round. I dropped flat just behind a wire fence and lay hoping it would soon cease. Any one who has been behind the line when one of these alarms are on know what it is, for nine out of ten shots find a billet behind the trenches. I just lay there listening to them singing all around me and occasionally hitting the wire fence about me, and expecting every moment to get one, and just wondering what part of me would be hit.

Anyhow there were none for me that time, and after about an hour of it, they dropped it off gradually. I did not wait for them to finish altogether, but set off and without meeting anyone, only two cows that were wounded and limping, I managed to get back to the road from where I started. I got behind a wall and had a rest and a smoke and started off again, saying to myself that this time I would be sure of every step. The best resolutions often miscarry for after half an hours walk I found myself astray again. I was properly tired of it now and made up my mind to go on no matter where I would finish up. So after climbing through some more wire and tearing my coat, besides falling in a Jack Johnson[63] hole, I landed on to a road, the direction of which I did not know. I resolved to go to the right and after a little while saw a small light coming from a house across the fields, so I decided to make for it, and after ploughing through two fields or quagmires, got to it. I found it was the

[63] A Jack Johnson was a heavy German artillery shell, named after a contemporary champion heavyweight boxer.

Head Quarters of the Norfolk Regt, which belonged to another Brigade.

I was pushed in before the Commanding Officer and the way they looked at me I thought they had taken me for a German. I would not have blamed them for I was not looking a very smart Britisher at the time, having more mud on me that was good for me. When I told them my Regiment, they were no wiser, but when I told them my Brigade and Division, the Adjutant said he thought they were on the right of his Battalion. He then drew a sketch on a piece of paper and explained the way I should go. I was put on my way a little and then struck off on my own. It was an awful road or path with little thin boards to walk over streams on, and mud up to your ankles. The fire along this part was a little hot and I thought I would not be sorry when I arrived at my own corps.

At last I came up to the trench and had to get into it along with the Norfolks for another fusillade was going. I discovered while there, that it was an advanced trench, with the Germans not 50 yards away. I thought our trenches bad, but this lot was ten times worse, being just waist deep and full of mud. One of their officers told me he would direct me and told me to wait a little by a stream and he would come back. I got a tree between myself and the enemy and was there about half an hour, during which I nearly got shot. One bullet went by my ear that close that it left my head singing, and another went into the tree behind me, so that I wasn't sorry when at last he turned up. He was with a party bringing some dead and wounded in, a party who had been on patrol. They had to move with the utmost caution here as they were practically on top of the enemy, and one of them asked me how far we were from the enemy. I said 200 yards, he said "When are you going to get closer and fight?" I said "Don't mention it, you never get any shell fire," and neither they did for being that close the artillery never fired on either side.

The officer then took me along with him and led me as far as a river on the right of his line. The reason I found out that they did not know our Regiment was their neighbour was with this river and our trenches lying a little back. When we got to the river he said he did not know for sure but he thought I could get across lower down and so he left me. I wandered up and down the bank of this river looking for some place to cross, but could find none, it being that dark. The enemy were now firing pretty hot as they do when the lines are close together, and I still kept looking up and down for some place to cross. There was a big tree, with a bough across, so I tried climbing across, but had to give it up, so I got that fed up at last that I took a firm hold of my blanket and jumped in. I had imagined it would not have been too deep to perhaps wade across, but I found myself going right down, so had to let go my blanket and start swimming. I was a good swimmer so did not think much of swimming in a full rig out, with big coat on and equipment, bayonet and ammunition.

I threw my cap across to the other side, making sure of that or the badge as they were so hard to get. There was a strong flow and I got carried down the river, a little too far I thought, towards the Germans for the bullets were coming mighty close again, and I was beginning to think I was not going to get out of this hole. I was unarmed and thought what a poor chance I would have, but then I had my bayonet and although it was wet it would do as a last resort. I managed at last to reach the bank and after a lot of struggling up the slimy bank got out, and got my cap lower down, but not my blanket and oilsheet. The Germans would get that as it would float that way.

I got to the left of our line in the finish and eventually, after a bit more mud plowing, arrived at my gun point. When I reported to my officer, he let me go back to get dried, so I set off to the lodge where I knew there would be a fire. On the limber in my pack I got a few dry things but had no trousers or coat, so had to lie up while they dried. It had been a very frosty night and if I had stood long in them I would have been stiff.'

The Quartermaster[64], T. E. Bunting DCM, was an old soldier with a fine record in the Regiment going back to the days of the campaign in the Sudan. As QM he always put the needs of the men first. On Christmas Eve 1914, this already twice-wounded soldier was promoted to Captain, and stayed with the Battalion throughout the war. His son, also called Thomas Edward, was commissioned into the Faughs on 25 April 1918, but was killed in action just four months later, and is buried at Bertenacre Military Cemetery.

A Christmas card sent by the Artists Rifles to the Faughs, Christmas 1914.

On Christmas Day the Battalion was billeted at La Crèche. It was a fine frosty morning, with services for the Roman Catholics being held in the village church and for Protestants in the schoolhouse. The Christmas cards sent by the King and Queen were distributed, together with Princess Mary's chocolate and cigarette boxes. Everyone had a good Christmas dinner thanks to gifts from home. Afterwards the Regimental Sergeant Major led some of the men in carol-singing around the village.

At the end of December an artillery observation officer was on duty in the trenches for the first time. It was only when he made his report that Divisional Headquarters realised the impunity with which the enemy was able to shell the Battalion positions.

On 29 December officers and NCOs[65] from the 2nd Battalion of the Faughs (part of the 27th Division) visited the 1st Battalion to learn about trench warfare. They saw at first hand the terrible effect the combination of the flooded River Douve, heavy rain and frosts had on the trenches.

On New Year's Eve the Germans in the trenches opposite got up on their parapets and waved to the Faughs to come over, so Captain G. V. W. Hill removed all badges of rank and went out into 'no man's land'. Two German soldiers informed him that there was a dead British soldier lying in front of their trench. Captain Hill asked the Germans to remove the identity disc and bury the soldier. The body proved to be that of 9162 Private R. Boyd[66], Royal Inniskilling Fusiliers. Captain Hill also discovered the identity of the two German units opposite and that the River Douve was the boundary between them. This was one of the many unofficial truces which happened spontaneously on many parts of the Western Front during the

[64] The Quartermaster or QM is the officer responsible to the Battalion Commanding Officer for all the movement, supplies, accommodation and maintenance of a military force.

[65] The ranks from Lance Corporal to Colour Sergeant are non-commissioned and by virtue of appointment. The rank of Sergeant Major is held by a Warrant from the Secretary of State. Officers from Second Lieutenant upwards are commissioned by the Sovereign.

[66] Pte Robert Boyd had served with the 2nd Battalion of the Inniskillings, and was killed on 1 November 1914. His grave has never been discovered and he is commemorated on the Ploegsteert Memorial.

During the truce of New Year's Eve 1914, Lt G. V. W. Hill (on the right) went across 'no man's land' to greet the Germans. On the left is Lt Henry.

Christmas and New Year of 1914. From 1915 onwards the British Army ordered that any further attempts at fraternisation would be considered a capital offence.[67]

When the 1st Battalion had left Shorncliffe it had comprised 23 officers and almost 1,000 other ranks. As 1914 drew to a close the Battalion recorded that 17 officers and 768 other ranks had been lost since the war started.

Sgt Wilson's journal continues:

'Wednesday the 23rd December came and it being our day for relief we were pleased as it left us out for Xmas. We marched to our farm

[67] An offence punishable by death, the word 'capital' deriving from the fact that execution was originally administered by means of decapitation.

of 5 miles distance and got billeted in the same place. The farmer at this house was very good, letting us have the kitchen at the back for cooking and for dining in. We now prepared to get it ready for having our Xmas dinner, and today the 24th I went with the empty limber into a large town close by for some spicy things to commemorate the day. One would have thought that we were in some large town in England for every where the streets were crowded with people buying for Xmas. The meat and fowl shops done well, being sold out for the most part.

The next day Friday was an ideal Xmas, the ground being covered with snow, and the morning was employed in getting good things given to us. Gifts of Christmas pudding, cigarettes and cakes we got in abundance and what with the parcels we got from home, we began to forget there was a war on at all. In the evening we had a little concert on our own in the kitchen and I managed to borrow a mandolin from a Frenchman, so that we had a little music also, not forgetting the French girls who came in with their gramophone. We did not understand the songs but the dance music we did and had a good time on the floor dancing. Afterwards I went with a troop under the Sgt Major, to all the different billets of the Companies in turn and gave them a little entertainment. We finished up in the Officers' Mess where we gave them a little extra and of course they saw we were well supplied with tobacco and drinks. We were all pleased at this time to see our King and Queen had not forgotten us, for we each received a present, the majority sending them home.[68]

The following day the snow vanished with a downpour of rain, letting us know our jollifications were at an end and we had some work in front of us for the New Year. After four days in this billet we left at 2.30 pm straight for the trenches, where we arrived about 6 pm. It was a good night, only for the rain which commenced again, being our usual luck in the trenches. When we were going up to the trenches it seemed quite strange to hear no shots going and all so quiet. It appears there had been a truce over Xmas, and the Jocks wanted us to keep it up and not start firing. They had been half way across and the Germans met them, exchanging papers etc. The Germans wanted to arrange a football match, but the Commanding Officer of the Seaforths would not allow it.

Their last words to the Jocks were, "Tell that mad Irish lot to keep quiet, they are always firing." So it can be imagined how quiet and unreal it was, not to have to keep our heads low and to be walking upright in the trenches. It was nothing uncommon to see men on either side walking about in daylight. It was a good thing for a party of civilians that it was like this, for one day a whole band of them came down the road until they could get no further. The walked right into our front line of trenches and were surprised to hear they could go no further. They had heard that the town in front which was in the hands of the Germans had been captured, and it being their native place were all flocking back to look after their shops etc. We sent an escort with them and conducted them back.

On another occasion a motor car mistook the way and came dashing along this road in full view of the enemy. There was no truce this time and the enemy let them get about half way when he opened fire. The chauffeur must have realised he was on the wrong road and turning round made off back at full speed, amidst a perfect hail of bullets. The car received a few, but he himself escaped which was lucky for him.

The artillery evidently had no thoughts of being amiable for they kept at it on both sides, and the following day we got a good shelling, every shell bursting in the right spot. Both sides knew the range to a yard. I, and my team,

[68] This was a brass box that contained either chocolate or cigarettes and tobacco. After the war these boxes were invariably used by the soldiers or their families to keep their campaign medals in.

were in another gun pit this time and had a couple of little dugouts just behind. These were only small, but we had made them fairly comfortable. In ours I had made a small fireplace, with a little spout of a chimney, which I had found in our old farm house just by. The enemy must have spotted it, although it was only sticking above ground about a foot, and they dropped two shells within a yard of it, and several more all around. I was in the trench in front at the time, and only got hit with mud. A little up the trench one shell went right through the top of a dugout, bursting inside and wounded six of our men all in the feet and legs. It was a good job they had not their heads the other way or it would have been all up with them. They said they had only changed round the day before.

The rain came on again, and made the trenches as bad as ever. The two following days were quiet, that quiet that some of the enemy came half way and beckoned us to meet them. We did not want to have anything to do with them, so long as they did not fire we would not, but at the same time orders were given to keep a stricter watch while on sentry, if that could be done. I saw one of our Corporals go to meet them and they remained talking for a while, and it was quite amusing to see the heads all along on both sides popping up to watch this affair in front. I heard a whistle sound and saw it was our CO signalling to the Corporal to come back, so they parted. When the Corporal came back the CO placed him under arrest for "having communication with the enemy". The Corporal was in a great state, and did not improve when he asked me what they would do on him, and I said they generally shot them. It was only a lesson for him, for he was let off afterwards.

On Thursday, the last day of the year, we got relieved again and this time went into Brigade Reserve, going to the farm behind the hill to our rear. I managed to get the kitchen again and we were badly in need of a fire for our ammunition belts could not be kept dry in the trenches. The four days that we spent here were wet days, and so we were indoors and glad to be there. On the night before we went back to the trenches we had a concert, which the troops enjoyed very much, especially as we had good music, having got a piano from the house.'

7
JANUARY TO MARCH 1915: FROSTBITE AND FEVER

The first few weeks of 1915 were comparatively quiet. Both sides had settled down to the routine of trench warfare, shelling, and raids. There was also the ever-constant need to repair and improve defences. The British supply of artillery shells had improved, in quantity and quality; now the Germans did not have it all their own way in barrages, and the ability to hit back greatly improved morale.

The greatest enemy was still the weather. The frequent snowfalls and frosts, then thaws, alternating with heavy rain, made living conditions

Only when in billets away from the front-line trenches did the soldiers have a chance to get properly clean.

in the trenches absolutely dreadful. The system of different units being rotated for service in the front-line trenches had now changed slightly, with men spending four days in the trenches, two in support and two further back behind the lines, in safe billets at La Crèche.

Greater attention was now paid to sanitation and hygiene in the trenches, with the result that, up to the end of January 1915, only 212 cases of enteric fever were reported in the British Army, and this was confined to soldiers who had not been inoculated. Massaging with whale oil continued to be very effective in preventing frostbite.

During the month of January, the 7th Argyll & Sutherland Highlanders joined the Brigade and were initiated into trench warfare, first by platoons, then by companies. They were a fine Territorial unit and acquitted themselves well both in trench warfare and later in the Second Battle of Ypres.

Lieutenant C. W. Sparks became the Faughs' Medical Officer, and together with his assistant, Sergeant H. W. Stoner, worked with maximum effort to aid the sick and wounded. When possible, Lieutenant Sparks sent officers and men to the Transport Lines for a few days rest. This brief respite saved the sanity of many soldiers.

On 27 January orders were received to form a grenadier platoon. This was to consist of 25 men from each company commanded by Second Lieutenant Cooke and one NCO. A grenadier was a soldier who was trained to throw grenades, a role for which height and strength was an advantage.

During the winter months there had been numerous reports of German spies operating behind the lines. Some of these were true, while many were not. On 31 January a Frenchwoman reported meeting a mounted patrol at Hill 63; she described the German uniforms and how they threatened to shoot her. Investigation proved that this was a British reconnaissance party scouting new artillery positions.

Describing events in January, Sgt Wilson's journal records:

> 'The next four days we were in the trenches, things were getting settled now, and we were getting accustomed to this kind of warfare. The usual toll of lives were taken and then out we would go to billet. One of the worst parts was to go out and come in, we having to pass along a main road not many hundreds of yards from the trenches. The enemy had this road marked well, for some one was always getting killed or wounded on it, and you never knew the moment machine gun fire would be opened on it. Luckily, there was a ditch on either side and many a time we had to fly into it, when we could hear the machine gun fire searching the road. We knew all the windy places on it and could tell the spot exactly where anything happened. You would hear so and so got killed last night. Where? Oh first there by the dead pig (a dead pig that had lain on the road for months), or by the dead cow or the Estaminet (an Inn). You can tell that whenever we got past these places we would heave a sigh of relief until we got to the next one. You could imagine at times that the enemy had taken deliberate aim, although it being dark, it could not have been so. I saw two men killed at once with the same bullet, passing exactly through the hearts of both of them. Occasionally our patrols would find the bodies of men lying out in front, which had been there for months, so that they were unrecognisable.[69]
>
> About the middle of January I was posted to an advanced position where I erected my gun. Originally it was the garden of the farm behind, or all of the farm that was left. There was a very small out house and a wall standing. In this position we were just a field away from the enemy, they being behind one hedge and

[69] When possible these bodies were carried back to British lines and given a suitable burial. The British soldiers' identity discs, which were only made of compressed card, did not usually survive either the cause of death or exposure, which left only regimental insignia or the chance of personal papers as a source to identity the body – hence the high number of gravestones in Western Front cemeteries inscribed with Rudyard Kipling's words, 'Known Unto God'.

we the other. The trench here was full of water, so that we could not remain in it, so we all, except the sentry who stood on a box, went into the little out house, in rear. The next day we were in this little house when the shelling commenced, one just lifting the thatch off, so we crawled to behind a little wall with a partial shelter over it. Here we remained all day, but it was just as bad, we got splashed all over with mud and water from a shell dropping in the pond a few feet away.

I remained here until Friday the 15th of January and this day we were as usual behind the little wall when two shells of ours in rapid succession just skimmed our shelter and fell in front a little without bursting. They must have been bad ones, and as we did not want to be put out with our own guns we shifted just before another couple came, even closer than the last. We crept across the yard to the small house we had been in before and were congratulating ourselves on arriving safe and unobserved, when the enemy commenced to shell us. We knew then that our movement had been seen, so there was nothing for it only to crouch on the floor and hope they missed us. It was warm though, for pieces were flying all round us, and when one bursted at the door, we thought it time to move somewhere else.

There was a trench behind, which had been abandoned and was half full of water, in which were some dugouts. We then decided to go for it and accordingly ran out for all we were worth. We got it though for they came that quick we had to drop down before we got round the corner. One piece of shell came down just between me and one of the men. He picked it up to show me what had just missed us, but dropped it quick as it was red hot. We could not lie here, so we up again and ran for the trench getting there alright, but having to go through a hail of bullets, for here we were in view of their trenches and they fired for all they were worth. They hit none of us thank goodness, so we scrambled through the trench up to our knees in water and succeeded in getting into an old dugout, which held the seven of us with a little squeezing. We were not to have it to ourselves though, for three men came down from the corner close by where we were, who were wounded, so we took them in and bandaged their wounds up.

One of my men was playing with an old trench rifle he had just found, when it suddenly went off, shooting a boy named Haddock.[70] It was unfortunate for he died a few days after. We could never get the men to be careful enough in the trenches with their rifles, any amount being killed accidentally. The Corporal who was speaking to the Germans got his arm shattered in this way, the shot killing another man before it hit him. At another time we lost two men at once with the same bullet, through a careless man with his rifle.

To resume – I could see that this poor fellow was done for and so I wished it would come dark, so the stretcher-bearers could take him off, but the guns stopped us again, they had evidently located our new abode. They were not far off either for as it grew dusk, the whole inside of the dugout would be lit up with the flashes of shells bursting overhead. It was very miserable sat here in our wet things and we were all wishing for dark to come, so that we could get out, and try and dry ourselves. We lost 16 killed and wounded in the corner of that trench that day.

At night as I was expecting I got word to go back to Headquarters for my papers to go on leave, and I was very pleased as one can imagine. I was rather late leaving owing to getting the wounded away, so that by the time I got back I had no time to change or do anything before I had to get away. There was a walk of about 4 miles to the bus which would take me to the railway station, leaving about 10 pm. I was home at 10 the following night. My leave was for eight days and it soon passed

[70] 11309 Pte Samuel Haddock, aged 19, was the son of George and Sarah Haddock, Union St, Lurgan, Co Armagh. He died of wounds on 27 January 1915 and is buried in Boulogne Eastern Cemetery.

and then on my way back to the trench again, where I arrived to find the Battalion in the trenches, due to get relieved the following day. I remained the night in one of the huts which had been erected behind the firing line, and found a change from being on leave.'

Despite adverse weather conditions most of February was spent in improving the trenches and defences. Most of the work was carried out during the hours of darkness and the Faughs were fortunate to have the assistance of Lieutenant Martell, of the 9th Field Company, Royal Engineers, an officer as brave as he was clever. The enemy attempted several attacks, but a combination of soft ground and deadly defences kept them at bay. Any movement across 'no man's land' was incredibly difficult in the mud, except when there was a hard frost, when the Battalion was always especially vigilant.

The Battalion came out of the trenches during the night of 5/6 March, so the Barrosa Day celebrations had to be held a day late when the Faughs reached their billets to the south of Hill 63. A letter describing the party atmosphere, written by Sgt S. G. Woolsey, was published in the *Armagh Guardian* on 2 April: 'I don't know much about the officers' part in it, but the NCOs and men enjoyed themselves. It was the first time that the sergeants had dined together since the war started. They congregated in a stable in La Courte Dreve Farm, with three tables in one of the stalls, and a good dinner (tomato stew), with tea, rolls, butter and sardines, some beer (of unknown nationality) and a gramophone on the table. You can imagine about forty sergeants sitting round the table, one of our own artists singing "When London Sleeps", and the guns rattling away outside, and you have got it all!'

The remnants of the Sergeants Mess of the 1st Battalion Royal Irish Fusiliers after 12 months of campaigning. They had embarked on 22 August 1914 with a strength of 57 – on 22 July 1915 only nine were left.

The other important occasion in the calendar of any Irish Regiment is St Patrick's Day. In 1915 the *Armagh Guardian* sent out sprigs of shamrock, and the Hon Mrs Gough sent the eatables: pea soup, roast beef, boiled ham, potatoes, plum pudding and cheese. The Artists Rifles[71] kindly organised the dinner and concert, which was to take place on 15 March at Bailleul. However, the war intervened and, with the Battle for Neuve Chapelle in the offing, the entire Battalion was transferred to Armentières. Not to be defeated, a company of the Artists Rifles trekked after the Faughs with not only the dinner, but also the crockery and tables. The Battalion was eventually presented with its shamrock and enjoyed the dinner on 16 March.

The concert given afterwards by the talented Artists Rifles would have done credit to any of London's music halls. With the Germans just a few

Right **A commemorative menu card for the St Patrick's Day and Barrosa Day celebrations of March 1915.**

Below **A simply and locally produced menu card for the St Patrick's Day celebrations in March 1915.**

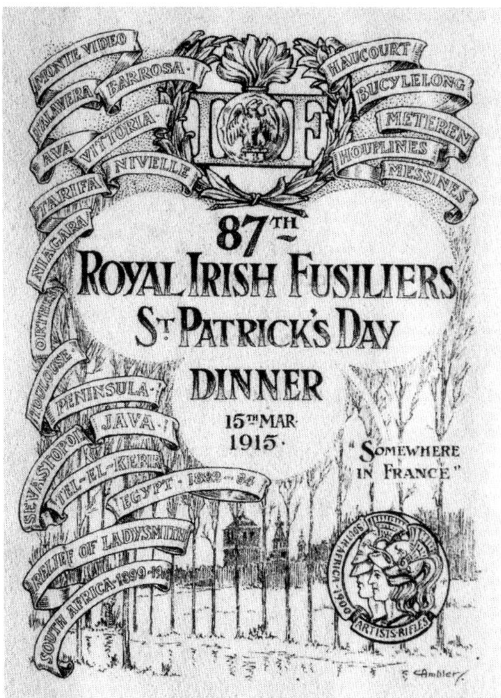

[71] This regiment was formed in 1859 by the eminent painter Lord Leighton PRA, and recruited artists, poets and musicians. As well as a fighting role during the First World War, the Artists Rifles set up training schools for officers in France and England, and organised and performed in concert parties for the troops. The war artists John and Paul Nash were both in the Artists Rifles, as was Wilfred Owen.

miles away, the usual enemy bombardment went on. As the 'Little Willies' and 'White Hopes'[72] landed close by, the French and American visitors were amazed at how the Irish troops could enjoy themselves.

The work of carrying up stores to the front line continued to be a laborious task. Dead cattle and other animals that had lain for some time were buried, including the half pig that had been a landmark on the Messines Road on dark nights. It was sorely missed!

British attacks were in progress further south, but the Douve Sector was quiet except for the Germans putting extra wire in front of their trenches. With the new trench maps, local names were quickly replaced with more familiar ones, and the various farms became known as Irish, Fusilier, Barrosa and Seaforth, the latter with its famous cellar.

During the rest of March the Battalion continued to move between its sector at Douve and the rest area at La Crèche. It also established a cemetery at Seaforth Farm, although it was completely

Lieutenants Carden-Roe (left) and Herrick standing on an improvised bridge over the moat that surrounded Seaforth Farm in the Douve Sector. The moat cut right through the 1st Battalion's trench line.

[72] 'Little Willies' was a derogatory reference to the German Kaiser, whose first name was Wilhelm. 'White Hope' referred to the former world champion heavy weight boxer Jim Jefferies, who was persuaded to come out of retirement in 1910 to fight the black heavyweight World Champion boxer Jack Johnson. Jefferies was dubbed the 'Great White Hope', but was knocked out in the 15th round. That shells were named after both of these boxers is a reference to the fact that, like their namesakes, they were 'heavyweights'.

obliterated by subsequent heavy fighting in this sector. The journal goes on:

'For the next couple of months we went in and came out of the trenches as before, getting shelled, losing men and wondering when we were going to have a move. Once during this time we were moved to attack at another part of the line and afterwards came back, having had a pleasant time in the town of Armentières where our Battalion was well known, it being the first to pass through and drive the Germans out. While there I took the opportunity to visit the policeman again, and found this time that they were all at home. He was very pleased to see me, saying he never expected to see me again, having seen a tomb stone or cross with my name on it.

We arrived back in our own trenches again and went into the usual routine of things. Our trenches were very good by now and we had plenty of room to move about, and we commenced to have fresh troops from home scattered amongst us to instruct them in the art of trench warfare. The days were nearly always the same now, shelling going on, sniping again, so that we had to be very careful not to expose ourselves too much. It was

From centre to right, some 'B' Company old hands, Pte Hill, Corporal Gilbert and Pte White, are seen in the trenches in the Douve Sector. In terms of living conditions the trenches had few home comforts, but were a vast improvement on the first trenches occupied by the Faughs near Frelinghien.

always exciting for in the day we would lie in our dugouts listening to the shells coming and bursting all round, finding some dugouts occasionally and we were hoping ours would be spared. Dawn found things lively for rifle fire was the order then until it got light, for at that time we would be stood to arms, and the same at dusk.

One morning at dawn we caught several snipers taking up their positions to annoy us during the day, and we gave them a volley, knocking some of them over, so we were not troubled that day with them, from that point anyhow. I had another couple of narrow escapes this time, one was when I was told off to find a billet for the section for that evening, as we were for relief. I went down by the communicating trench, and when I came to the road I took the wrong way and in the end had to get out on the main road and run until I got under cover. They let me have it though and I was lucky to get out of it. The second occasion was in the trench when one of our chaps called my attention to the German trench in front which had a white target up on a stick for us to pass our time away shooting at it. I got up and took a steady shot at it and hit it I believe for I seen it shake. Anyhow, he signalled me up a hit, and I was taking another steady aim when a bullet whistled past my eyes, striking the sandbag at my face and ripping it open. I am sure another fraction would have got me, for it stunned me slightly, so that I dropped down into the trench. I could not see for a little and when I took my hands from my face they were all blood, so I made sure I was hit. I was lucky for my face was only cut slightly and scratched all over. The small stones and grit out of the sandbag had done it. I wanted no more shots there.

This was only one of their ways to catch us, for while the target was up in the trench, a sniper was concealed in front watching for who would be fool enough to fire at it. They did not get it all their own way, for about the same place we were always getting annoyed by snipers and one day we thought we saw a slight movement and fired at it. It was a sniper alright, and when he saw that he was caught on, he up and ran, but he never got back. Towards the end of stay in the trenches things became very lively, we would be bombarded all day almost and were constantly "standing to". With the zig-zag position of the trenches we used to get fired on from all directions, losing any amount of men, who would be shot in the back of their heads and bodies.'

8
April 1915: slaughter at St Julien, the Second Battle of Ypres

As Easter approached, the Faughs were still in the routine of moving between La Crèche and the Douve Sector. A welcome distraction was a supply of free newspapers from home. While all battalions now had grenadier platoons, they were still using improvised bombs or grenades made by packing explosives into jam tins with a nerve-testing 3-second fuse. In April the latest improvisation was to use catapults to throw the bombs to a maximum of 40 yards.

On 11 April there was a lot of enemy activity both in the air and on the ground with the shelling of the Chateau of La Hutte, on Hill 63.

The next day was to be the Faughs' last in the Douve Sector, and it proved to be an eventful one. In addition to the normal bombardment the Germans opened fire with much heavier artillery. The first shells burst north-west of Dead Cow Farm and, aided by excellent observation posts on Messines Ridge, the range was systematically shortened until the shells were landing in the trench south of the River Douve. When on target the guns proceeded to demolish the trench foot by foot.

It was on this occasion that Private Robert Morrow of 'D' Company won the Victoria Cross for his conspicuous bravery and devotion to duty. The award was notified in the *London Gazette* of 22 May 1915, in the following words:

> 'For most conspicuous bravery near Messines on April 12th, 1915, when he rescued and carried successfully to places of comparative safety, several men who had been buried in the debris of trenches wrecked by shell fire. Private Morrow carried out this gallant work on his own initiative, and under very heavy fire from the enemy.'

Private Morrow died of wounds received on 25 April 1915, during the Second Battle of Ypres. The late Tsar of Russia also awarded him the Medal of St George, Third Class. The following were also recommended for gallantry at Second Ypres: Lieutenant Sparks RAMC, Second Lieutenant Henry (attached), Sergeant Donaldson, who had been severely wounded, Sergeant Thomas, and Bandsman (Lance Corporal) Fincham.

During the night of 12 April the Battalion was relieved by the Warwickshires and marched via Ploegsteert, Romerin and Robat to billets in Bailleul, arriving at 2.30am on the 13th. Just before they arrived Bailleul was bombed by a Zeppelin[73].

The following three days were spent in

[73] Count Ferdinand von Zeppelin built his first airship in 1900. A huge cigar-shaped bag with an internal aluminium framework was filled with highly flammable hydrogen gas. In the five-year period before the First World War, Zeppelin's airships made some 1,588 flights, carrying 34,228 passengers a total of some 170,000 miles. So successful were his designs that the word 'zeppelin' became synonymous with powered airships. Zeppelin continued improving his designs throughout the First World War, building 88 for military use, many of them being used in bombing raids over Great Britain and the Western Front. The airships could maintain higher altitudes than any of the aeroplanes then available and were therefore largely invulnerable to Allied fighter planes.

comparative luxury. The mornings were taken up with training, the grenadiers practising with the new rifle grenade, and the afternoons were devoted to sports. The locals welcomed the British soldiers into their homes. By the end of the war the entire town was reduced to rubble, and subsequently the people of Bailleul transformed the remains of their church into one of the most impressive and emotive of French war memorials.

On 16 April the Battalion marched 4 miles to new billets in the village of Merris. Again the Faughs got on well with the locals and used the regimental transport to bring up materials to repair their damaged church. The village was destroyed in the spring of 1918 and was one of those that marked the limit of the German advance.

This week of rest and relaxation marked the lull before the storm, or what the soldiers called the 'fattening process'. They were being prepared for a major attack, which turned out to be the taking of Frelinghien. The Commanding Officer and the Company Commanders were taken on buses to reconnoitre their old lines near Houplines.

On 20 April all companies visited the battlefield of Méteren, where they had fought on 13th October 1914. There were few visible traces of the fight, and the men took the opportunity to put the grave of Second Lieutenant Samuels[74] in good order.

In that month Sgt Wilson recorded:

> 'At the beginning of April we got word that our Division was to be relieved for a rest awhile in some remote spot far away. We were all pleased at this news and when a week later we were marching out, we were in the best of spirits. We had lain in these trenches for about five months, and there being no active work, it was getting a little slow for a regular division, especially as plenty of Territorials were now about. Our trenches were taken over by a Territorial Division, so we were to be given a rest and then into some part where there was a little more life. Our Battalion was to be billeted for a few days in Bailleul, a large town a few miles back, and as usual several were sent on ahead to take over the billets, draw the rations etc for their respective Companies. I was one of these and secured good billets for the section, in three houses in a small court yard. In one of these was a very old man who had been in the Franco Prussian War of 1870. He and his wife lived alone and he had had soldiers billeted on him before and asked me if I could manage to let him off this time, saying he would find me a bed. So as there was any amount of room for them all, I took the bed and sleeping on a spring bed was quite a change.
>
> This night I was in the town about four hours before the Battalion arrived. During this time it was dark and we were honoured by a visit from the Zeppelins. It was quite exciting while it lasted, being a new experience for most of us. We would see the Zepps[75] quite plain, as they were flying low. About a score of bombs were dropped, and a number of places wrecked. I got a good shaking, being near to a house which was smashed up by one. All the civilians inside were killed, these being mostly women. As they left they gave us a shower of bullets from a machine gun, and we could hear them rattling off the slates of the houses above us. We had three days in this town and enjoyed ourselves very much, being allowed to go about wherever we wished.'

At 11.15am on 23 April orders were received to prepare to move north immediately. The Germans had attacked to the north-east of Ypres, and, using gas for the first time, they had overwhelmed the French troops and driven them, together with the civilian population, to the western bank of the Yser Canal. The British left flank was exposed and reinforcements were desperately needed to hold the line and prepare a counter-attack. The Faughs set off at 8.20pm, marching via Bailleul and arriving at their billets at Dranoutre at 11.30pm.

---

74 Lt Arthur M. Samuels had been killed when the Faughs had captured the ridge north of Méteren on 13 October 1914. He was from Kingstown, Dublin, and was aged 25 when he died. He is buried at Méteren Military Cemetery.

75 Zeppelin airships

At 7.15 the next morning they were on the move again, and after a short rest at Locre they marched on to Zevecoten, eventually reaching Ouderdom at 4.30pm. Here extra hand grenades and carriers were issued, together with another 100 rounds of ammunition per man and two sandbags.

The journal continues:

'Orders came for to march to a small village about four miles away, so it seemed they were giving us a touch of both town and country before they plunged us into it again. Our billets in this new place were very nice, only I had no spring bed this time. We spent a week here, and passed a very quiet and pleasant time. The mornings being occupied in performing drill just to keep fit and the afternoons and evenings we had to ourselves. We were firing our guns one morning on a small range we had fixed up, when orders came to get ready to move at a moment's notice. We got our final orders about 4 pm, when we marched off and only stopped to rest about midnight and the next morning were on our way again, passing Hill 60 and coming to a halt just below Ypres. Here we halted and were issued out with flare lights, the Companies with bombs, sandbags, picks and shovels etc. So by these preparations we knew we were for something good.'

The Battalion reached its rendezvous at the crossroads about 3,000 yards to the east of Vlamertinghe at 7.15pm. The men rested by the roadside while the officers sheltered in a nearby dressing station. As darkness fell the scene was typical of the chaotic rear area of any battlefield. The Ypres-Poperinghe road, which normally took four streams of traffic, was now crowded with ammunition and supply wagons going forward. Going in the opposite direction were hurrying ambulances and wounded men, each with their own account of the battle. Exhausted soldiers slept by the roadside, oblivious to the noise of marching feet, clattering wheels or exploding shells. The

One of three well-preserved German concrete blockhouses in the village of St Julien.

whole scene was illuminated by flames from the burning town of Ypres.

Rain was falling as the Faughs got on the move again by midnight. Their route took them north past 'Salvation Corner'[76] amid enemy shelling. During a brief halt at the village of Saint Jean, in a small cottage, its roof burst open by a shell, the Brigadier issued his orders for the attack. The situation was confused, but it was believed that the Canadians still held the village of St Julien[77]. The Faughs were to go to their assistance.

At 3.15am on 25 April, the following orders were issued. The first objective was to link up with the Royal Dublin Fusiliers north of Fortuin, to form an east-west line with the left flank at Hanebeek. The second objective was to fill the gap of about 500 yards between St Julien and the Suffolk Regiment east of Hanebeek.

Units were detailed as follows: 'C' Company under Captain Elkan was to form a firing line on the left; 'D' Company under Captain Jeudwine was to link with the Suffolks on the right; 'A' Company under Major Kentish and the Machine Gun Section under Lieutenant Herrick were to support 'C' Company; and Captain Bull's 'B' Company was Battalion reserve and support for 'D' Company and to protect the exposed right flank.

The road was choked with wounded and transport wagons and a misty dawn was breaking by the time the Battalion left the village of Wieltje. From the increasing sound of rifle and machine gun fire it was obvious that the enemy still held the farms between there and St Julien.

Back to the journal:

> 'Marching off again at dark, we halted again on the left of Ypres. It was dark now and we lay down by the road and tried to sleep. There were a number of buildings in Ypres on fire, so that the whole place was lit up, and we could hear the German shells still bursting among the buildings. I managed to doze off, but very soon got called up and we were on the way once more, and after marching a little way our transport remained behind, also our limbers, so we got the guns out and carried them, knowing now that we had not very far to go. As we were going up the rise on to the level above, dawn broke, when we emerged on the plain we came under rifle fire. There had been heavy fighting here the day before as we could see by the bodies lying about.
>
> There was a stretch of about half a mile up to the enemy's position and our troops were advancing in the fastly gathering light across this. I sometimes think if we had moved half an hour earlier and it not so light we would not have lost so heavily. As we went on our Division could be seen advancing to the attack all along, but we had no time to watch them for we had to get on ourselves.'

Disorientated by the explosions, gunfire and rising casualties, the Commanding Officer mistook a small stream for the River Hanebeek and deployed the companies too far to the rear. As the sections were moving along the shallow roadside ditches the Royal Dublin Fusiliers were spotted already deployed some distance ahead and to the east. The mistake was quickly corrected and the deployment completed, with the following changes: three machine guns were sent with 'C' Company, and 'A' Company took the place of 'B' Company as Battalion reserve.

The Battalion advanced to the attack at 6am, without any artillery support, and faced with heavy machine gun fire. Half an hour later losses had been severe and the advance ground to a halt just 70 yards short of St Julien village. Battalion

[76] Named after a Salvation Army hut that stood at a junction in Ypres. The Salvation Army provided food, accommodation and comfort for the soldiers in many towns along the Western Front throughout the First World War, a service they still provide today. This tradition was maintained when their mobile canteen served tea and buns to the Second World War veterans at the Dedication of the Memorial Garden at Caen on 5 June 2004.

[77] In fact, after a gas attack and a gallant defence by the Canadians, the Germans captured St Julien on 24 April 1915. By June 1917 the Germans had completed their lines of concrete blockhouses in the area, three of which can still be seen today. The Allies finally recaptured St Julien on 3 August 1917.

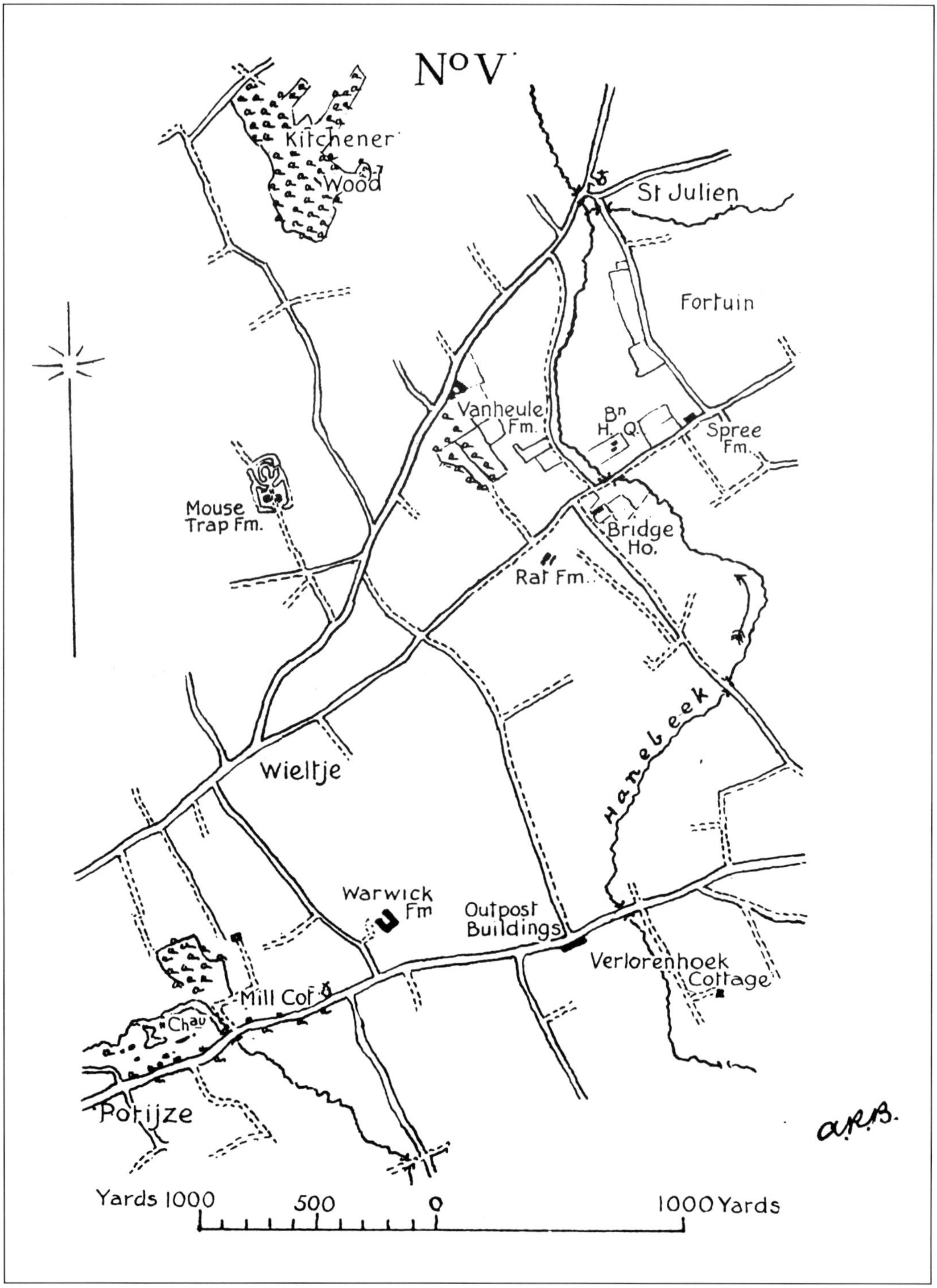

Map showing the area around St Julien village, near Ypres.

The long gradual incline devoid of cover that became the killing slopes for the Faughs at St Julien.

Headquarters had been set up in a farm at the point where the River Hanebeek met the Wieltje road, with good views of the battlefield. From there at about 6.30am, British troops were seen withdrawing from Kitchener's Wood[78]. The retreat, caused by British shells falling among their own troops, spread to the right, eventually reaching the Faughs on the extreme right of the attack.

However, the forward lines of the Royal Irish Fusiliers did not retire, for they lay dead on the slope in front of St Julien. Sgt Wilson continues:

> 'A machine gun attachment went forward as a unit of its own with our Officer in charge. We advanced from cover to cover, extended out as if a Company carrying our guns and ammunition, for had the enemy known we were machine gunners, every rifle would have been turned on us. We kept going forward amid a very heavy rifle fire until we got into a shallow ditch close up to the enemy, when our officer got hit in the chin. I was next to him and put a bandage on him and said "Lie down", but he got up and staggered off to find the dressing station. I, being the next senior, was then in charge, so I ordered the advance, and we rushed across an open space until we came to a hedge round a farm house. Here there was hardly any cover so that it was a very unhealthy spot. Some of the Dublins were behind the hedge to our left and they were getting slaughtered wholesale, the enemy being only a few yards away. This hedge finished a little to the right and so I told the next senior I was going to creep along to see if I could find a position for our guns. The bullets were coming through this hedge like hail, and as I crept along I had to crawl over the dead bodies of some of the Dublins.

[78] Just 1km from St Julien, Kitchener's Wood is now an open field, but was the scene of very heavy fighting in 1915.

When I got to the corner I saw that one of ours had been there before for he was lying dead by a tree, so I kept low and had a look around. I could see the Germans bobbing up and shooting just a few yards away and then a party of Dublins charged and it was quite lively watching them shooting and stabbing them. They captured the trenches to our front, but the trenches on our right were still in possession of the enemy. I forgot myself watching this affair, and when I looked round I saw my men all up running to a trench a little to the left. I shouted to them and the other Sgt shouted they had been ordered there. So I was left on my own, and being in command of the guns I had no rifle, and oh I so wished I had one for there was a German bobbing about, that looked an extra good target.'

'A' Company under Major Kentish formed a rallying point for men of all corps who could reach him. Their retreat was covered by a few Faughs who held the bed of the Hanebeek River in a last-ditch action before being taken prisoner.

About 8.30am the Battalion had established a line running from the Battalion Headquarters to near Vanheule Farm, which was held by the Royal Dublin Fusiliers. The soldiers dug in furiously with

Sgt Paul Radmilovic (on the left) from Cardiff, who had joined the Royal Irish Fusiliers in 1907, was killed at St Julien on 25 April 1915.

their entrenching tools trying to get some cover from the continuous shellfire.

The problem was now the right flank, where the Suffolks should have been. But they had been pushed back some distance to the right rear, their position uncertain from minute to minute. Just as the Germans were about to launch a counter-attack the Territorials of the Northumbrian Division threw themselves heroically into the fray, incurring terrible losses.

Losses to the Faughs were also severe, and made worse by the fact that those men who would normally have served in the rear had come forward to join in the attack. The attack had been a failure. To expect a single battalion with only four machine guns and no artillery support to take a strongly defended village was sheer madness. Nevertheless, the Faughs had done well and had nothing to be ashamed of. Losses that day for the Faughs were three officers killed and seven wounded, 45 Other Ranks killed, 160 wounded and 150 missing (most of whom were actually dead). Captain Penrose was one of the many who were listed as missing.

The fate of this popular officer, who had demonstrated his bravery in every action he had been in and who had been recommended for a gallantry award, remained a mystery until 1919. In December of that year, his father, the Rev John T. Penrose, received some papers belonging to his son from a German professor at Aachen, which the latter had found in a dugout on the River Hanebeek on 25 April 1915, indicating that though wounded he had made it back to the dugout. If, as is likely, he was removed from there as a casualty, without those papers his body was unidentifiable. Meanwhile, Sgt Wilson was in difficulties:

Captain Edward John McNeill Penrose was also killed in action at St Julien on that day. He has no known grave and is commemorated on the Ypres (Menin Gate) Memorial.

> 'My plan now was to get to the trench where the remainder were and so I commenced to crawl back again. While I was going along one of the Dublins came along who had been shot through the head, just above the eyes. I lay there looking at him for a good while amazed to know how he was living, but it soon brought me back to myself when he asked to be bandaged up and what was the best way to get back. I said across the open was the only way I knew, but he would be shot again if he tried that way, better to lie here. He would not, however, for he up and ran across and the last I saw of him was going across the fields for all he was worth.
>
> I thought it about time now that I got up and ran for the trench, little thinking it would be my last run. So I up and ran and had only got a short distance when I felt a sharp stinging blow in my knee, and it came suddenly to me I had been shot. I ran on a few paces more when I found myself unable to do any more, and by good luck I espied a shell hole just in front and with one last effort dived into it. When I got in I found it did not half cover me from view, but my first thought was

This shell hole, now water-filled, still exists in the section allocated to the Faughs to attack on 25 April 1915. It was in a shell hole like this that Sgt Hugh Wilson sheltered for 12 hours as the battle raged around him.

to see to my wound, for I could feel the blood running from it. I got my bandage out and after a lot of wriggling I managed to somewhat bind it up. My next thought was to get further down in this hole, especially as my feet were showing and I could hear bullets spitting into the ground just by them. I knew that the same German was still having a go at me.'

The darkness brought no rest for the exhausted troops, who had to consolidate their present position and stay alert to German counter-attacks. The war diary describes the next few days as 'a continuous nightmare'. Day merged with night as the soldiers worked feverishly to dig in and straighten the line. The Germans bombarded the line during the day, but at night shelled the roads to stop supplies being brought up or the wounded from being evacuated. Meanwhile, for Sgt Wilson:

'There was nothing to dig with only my bayonet, so with bayonet and hands I laboured on, digging it with the bayonet and throwing it out with my hands. At last I had to stop for I had got just under cover and I was getting done up with loss of blood, for when I looked there was a big pool of it by my knee. I got my towel from my haversack and bound it on top, as tight as I could, but it soon came through this and I began to think I would die from loss of blood before night came and I was picked up. I did not expect to get away before, as no one could come near. So I lay that day through, wishing night would come, and all the time shells were bursting all about, so that I began to think I was to have another one. It was a good thing I had some water in my bottle, for if not I am sure I would have died this day. I should say it was about eight in the morning when I got hit and it was eight at night when I eventually got picked up.

I was shouting and an officer of the Dublins heard me and came and lifted me out and threw me across his back. This was agony but I did not say anything, but when he went a few steps and fell in a ditch with me, I could not help but roar as I came down full on my leg. The Germans heard me I am sure. He said "Poor fellow" and said he would send some men with a stretcher for me, so I was left again. After a while, which seemed eternity, three men came, but no stretcher so they carried me on two rifles on which I sat. I went through torture again with this and when eventually I got in the van I was glad, although I and another man below me were giving an occasional roar as it bumped over a stone or jogged over a hole in the road, and by the way it was full of these.

After about an hour in this van we were taken out into the 1st Field Hospital, and after getting dressed were laid out to wait for vans to take us to the Railway station. I was in a big room along with many more, and there were plenty worse than me. The orderlies would come in and take one out who had died, and they were in often for they were dying quick. I lay in this hospital for about three hours when I was removed along with others by motor to the station. During the time I was in this hospital the enemy shelled some building close by, for when every time one of these large shells burst it shook so much that it broke the windows where I was in and the orderlies removed the stretchers into the centre of the room. This was to prevent the glass falling on us.'

During the night of 25/26 April a weak battalion of the Royal Irish Regiment commanded by Colonel G. M. Gloster mistakenly dug in to the front right of the Faughs. This mistake was rectified the following night, when the Royal Irish lengthened the line to the right of the Faughs, filling the gap between the 10th and 11th Brigades.

The next day two attacks were launched against the enemy line, first by the Lahore Division then by a brigade of the Northumberland Fusiliers, but neither achieved much, except more casualties.

At about 9am on the 27th the Germans were seen massing in the direction of St Julien, but they did not attack. A French attack delivered further north in the afternoon met with success.

On 28 April a German aircraft was brought down close to the Brigade headquarters. A cemetery was established there and soldiers of several units, including Lieutenant Lynden-Bell, were buried there in a common grave marked by a wooden cross. In 1917 Captain A. R. Burrowes revisited the spot, then only recognisable by a plank road and a muddy ditch. By good luck he spotted a rotten piece of wood with 'Bell' on it. He had a more substantial cross put up and after the Armistice the bodies were removed.[79]

Lt Donald Lynden-Bell (left), killed in action, aged only 19, at St Julien on 25 April 1915.

[79] Lt Donald Perceval Lynden-Bell from Basingstoke in Hampshire was only 19 when he was killed in action at St Julien. He is now buried at New Irish Farm Cemetery.

The grave of Lt Lynden-Bell at New Irish Farm Cemetery. His family had his gravestone inscribed 'Fell in the attack on St Julien leading his men'.

A draft of 50 men joined the Battalion on 29 April, bringing the ration strength up to 453 all ranks, approximately half the normal strength of a battalion. Such had been the price paid by the 1st Battalion Royal Irish Fusiliers in just eight months.

'After a week in Boulogne during which I went under an operation and had the bullet removed from my leg, I was sent to England and placed in Netley hospital. Enough of this, for after nine months here, during which time I underwent six operations and took enough chloroform to put a German Brigade out, I was discharged from the Army, being no longer fit for service.

Not fit for service means in my case not fit for civil employment, for my leg still troubles me and I cannot walk much. I am now destined to end my existence on a few shillings per week, which the Government has graciously allowed me.

There are numerous incidents which I have failed to mention as it would be impossible to describe it correctly, such as how I used to prowl about in the day time, climbing into the roofs of houses to watch our artillery fire on the enemy and how one day I went into a cottage and tried to get up in the loft through the trap door and how when I pushed, it seemed as if someone was holding it down and later another Sgt and I chased the supposed spy with our rifles but being dark he got away. How on another occasion a spy was caught dressed as a Lance Corporal and being questioned by the sentry said he was an Officer's servant, which of course gave him away as a Non Commissioned Officer would not be. How on another occasion a German came across to our trench who was drunk and shouted "Komarade", bring a bottle of beer for his "Komarades" to drink, and how we put him in a barrow as he could hardly walk and how as he was taken back to Headquarters he was thrown out at every pool of mud that came in the way, so that when the Officer saw him, one could not say whether he was a man or a sack of mud. Any how, the information that was got out of him, led to our artillery one night firing into some farm houses in which he said they went to billet on certain nights.

There are many more such incidents and I could go on writing, but I think enough has been said by a one time Sergeant in the Regular Army.

Sgt H. Wilson'

Colours that **never** run!

The Old Contemptibles

In 1964 the Royal Irish Fusiliers Museum appealed for First World War veterans from the Regiment to send in photographs and their stories.

These are some of the heroes.

Opposite page, left to right, from top row RSM G. A. Williams MM; Pte J. McCormick; 10538 Sgt J. Lawlor; 11213 Pte E. Hardy; 4703 Pte W. J. Doak from Belfast, who joined the Faughs on 11 November 1893; Pte T. Devlin; 2/Lt William Carden-Roe, who was later awarded the Military Cross, Mentioned in Despatches three times, and served with distinction during the Second World War; Pte S. Bradley; and Pte J. Forsythe.

This page, left to right, from top row CSM Walter C. Clark; Lt D. L. Allen, who also served in the Royal Flying Corps; Lt M. J. W. O'Donovan; 11332 Cpl A. Turkington, who gained the rank of Lt Colonel in the Home Guard during the Second World War, and later served as the County Commandant in the Ulster Special Constabulary for Down, being awarded the OBE in 1956; Captain Geoffrey M. H. Wright; Pte Halliday; 10454 Cpl M. O'Neill; Lt C. S. Tuely, who returned the Regimental Colours to Armagh in August 1914; and Pte W. Mallaghan.

ROLL OF HONOUR, 1ST BATTALION ROYAL IRISH FUSILIERS, AUGUST 1914 TO APRIL 1915

The following are the officers and men who served with Sgt Hugh Wilson and who were killed during the period covered by his journal. Many more were killed from this and the other battalions of the Royal Irish Fusiliers during the rest of the war. The complete Roll of Honour is held at the Royal Irish Fusiliers Museum.

During my research in the Regimental archives I found several soldiers whose death was unknown to the Commonwealth War Graves Commission. It is hoped that their sacrifice will soon be recognised and their names added to the Memorials on the Western Front.

Adamson George, Private, No 6105
Born in Portadown, County Armagh, resided in Belfast, enlisted in Portadown. He was killed in action on 25 April 1915 at St Julien. He has no known grave and is commemorated at the Ypres (Menin Gate) Memorial.

Alderman, Frank, Private, No 9634
Born, resided and enlisted in Winchester. He was killed in action on 12 April 1915 at Armentières. He has no known grave and is commemorated at the Ploegsteert Memorial.

Allison, William, Private, No 7864
Born in Ballymena, County Antrim, enlisted in Belfast, resided in Drogheda, County Louth. He died at home on 14 November 1914. He is named on the Ballymena War Memorial. He has no known grave and will be commemorated at the United Kingdom 1914-1918 Memorial, Brookwood, Surrey.

Anderson, Thomas, Private No 8760
He was killed in action on 21 March 1915 at Armentières. He has no known grave and is commemorated at the Ypres (Menin Gate) Memorial.

Armstrong, William Henry, Lance Corporal, No 7599
Born, resided and enlisted in Portadown, County Armagh. He was killed in action on 11 March 1915 near Armentières. He has no known grave and is commemorated at the Ploegsteert Memorial.

Baker, John, Private, No 6796
Born in Dundalk, County Louth, enlisted in

Dublin, resided in Potton, Bedfordshire. He was killed in action on 18 October 1914 near Houplines. He is buried at Houplines Communal Cemetery Extension.

Ball, John David Sullivan Leonard, Lance Sergeant, No 9869
Born in Chatham, enlisted in Dublin, and resided in Tunbridge Wells, Kent. He died of wounds on 3 October 1914 No 5 Stationary Hospital Advanced Base. He is buried at Le Mans West Cemetery.

Bartley, Michael, Private, No 8579
Born in County Donegal, enlisted in Glasgow, and resided in Newferry, Cheshire. He died of wounds on 15 October 1914 at French Military Hospital at St Omer. He is buried at Longuenesse (St Omer) Souvenir Cemetery.

Barton, James, Private, No 11709
Born in Ardee, County Louth, enlisted in Edinburgh, resided in Leith. He was killed in action on 25 April 1915. He has no known grave and is commemorated at the Ypres (Menin Gate) Memorial.

Barugh, Thomas William, Private, No 7919
Born in Bombay, India, and enlisted in Leeds. He died of wounds on 27 August 1914 at St Quentin. He is buried at St Souplet British Cemetery.

Bell, Charles, Lance Corporal, No 8256
He was killed in action on 25 April 1915 at St Julien. He has no known grave and is commemorated at the Ypres (Menin Gate) Memorial.

Bell, Moses, Private, No 5760
Born and resided in Dollingstown, County Down, and enlisted in Lurgan, County Armagh. He was killed in action on 25 April 1915 at St Julien. He has no known grave and is commemorated at the Ypres (Menin Gate) Memorial.

Bew, C. G., Private, No 9329
He was killed in action on 26 October 1914 at Houplines. He is buried at Houplines Communal Cemetery Extension.

Boughton, Albert, Private, No 10936
Born and resided in Drumcondra, Dublin, and enlisted in Dublin. He died of wounds on 27 April 1915 at No 10 Casualty Clearing Station. He is buried at Hazebrouck Communal Cemetery.

Boyle, Henry, Private, No 10309
Born in Belfast, resided in Castlerea, County Roscommon, and enlisted in Cavan. He was killed in action on 18 October 1914 near Houplines. He is buried at Houplines Communal Cemetery Extension.

Brigdell, Gerald George, Private, No 11393
Born in Limerick, resided in Glasgow, and enlisted in Hamilton, Lanarkshire. He was killed in action on 23 November 1914 at Nieppe. He has no known grave and is commemorated at the Ploegsteert Memorial.

Brophy, George, Private, No 9339
Born, resided and enlisted in Dublin. He was killed in action on 17 September 1914 near Bucy-le-Long. He has no known grave and is commemorated at La Ferté-sous-Jouarre Memorial.

Bryan, Daniel, Private, No 11302
Born and Resided in Kingstown, County Dublin, and enlisted in Dublin. He died of wounds on 26 April 1915 at No 2 Clearing Hospital, Bailleul. He is buried at Bailleul Communal Cemetery and Extension.

Burke, Edward, Private, No 6240
Born in Hulme, Manchester, resided at Old Trafford, Manchester, and enlisted in Manchester. He was killed in action on 25 April 1915 at St Julien. He has no known grave and is commemorated at the Ypres (Menin Gate) Memorial.

Burns, Samuel, Private, No 11122
Born and resided in Bessbrook, County Armagh, and enlisted in Newry. He was originally listed as missing and was accepted as having been killed in action on 27 August 1914, by the War Office on 20 January 1916. In his will he wrote, 'In the event of my death, I give all my love to all I leave behind. That's about all I can do, so they can go to the bank and draw. I leave breath and my money. They can spend it anyway.' He has no known grave and is commemorated at La Ferté-sous-Jouarre Memorial.

Byrne, John, Private, No 7654
Born, resided and enlisted in Dublin. He was originally listed as missing and was accepted as having been killed in action on 25 April 1915, by the War Office on 5 October 1916. He has no known grave and is commemorated at the Ypres (Menin Gate) Memorial.

Byrne, Patrick, Private, No 6252
Born, resided and enlisted in Dublin. He also served in the Boer War. He was killed in action on 25 April 1915 at St Julien. He has no known grave and is commemorated at the Ypres (Menin Gate) Memorial.

Byrne, William Joseph, Private No 11265
Born, resided and enlisted in Dublin. He was killed in action on 18 October 1914 near Houplines. He is buried at Houplines Communal Cemetery Extension.

Carbery, Miles Bertie Cunninghame, Captain
Son of the late Mr and Mrs W. E. Carbery of Hartington Mansions, Eastbourne. Husband of Elizabeth Dora Carbery of 'Ringmore', Connaught Road, Camberley. He was killed in action on 18 October 1914. He is buried at Houplines Communal Cemetery Extension.

Carmichael, Andrew, Private No 8318
Born and resided in Ballyclare, County Antrim, and enlisted at Belfast. He was killed in action on 25 April 1915 at St Julien. He has no known grave and is commemorated at the Ypres (Menin Gate) Memorial.

Carson, William, Private, No 5749
Born and resided in Dollingstown, County Down, enlisted in Lurgan, County Armagh. He died of wounds on 27 April 1915 at No 10 Field Ambulance. He is buried at Vlamertinghe Military Cemetery.

Carty, Edward, Lance Corporal, No 7074
Born, resided and enlisted in Dublin. He was killed in action on 18 October 1914 near Houplines. He is buried at Houplines Communal Cemetery Extension.

Chambers, Bernard, Private, No 5316
Born, resided and enlisted in Newry, County Down. He was originally listed as missing and was accepted as having been killed in action on 25 April 1915 at St Julien, by the War Office on 18 September 1916. He has no known grave and is commemorated at the Ypres (Menin Gate) Memorial.

Cheney (or Cheyne), Edward Emerson, Private, No 8409
Born in Enniskillen, resided in Belfast, and enlisted in Glasgow. He was killed in action on 25 April 1915 at St Julien. He has no known grave and is commemorated at the Ypres (Menin Gate) Memorial.

Clanachan, James, Private, No 8412
Born in Dundrum, County Dublin, resided in Blacklion, County Cavan, and enlisted in Newry, County Down. He was killed in action on 7 December 1914 at Douve near Armentières. He has no known grave and is commemorated at the Ploegsteert Memorial.

Clarke, William, Private, No 5598
Born in Bessbrook, County Armagh, resided in Newry, County Down, and enlisted in Armagh. He was killed in action on 7 December 1914 near Armentières. He has no known grave and is commemorated at the Ploegsteert Memorial.

Cleary, William, Private, No 11016
Born in Forfar, resided in Dundee and enlisted in Hamilton. He died of wounds on 19 October 1914 at Armentières. He has no known grave and is commemorated at the Ploegsteert Memorial.

Coffey, Peter, Private, No 9636
Born in Multyfarnham, County Westmeath, resided in Rathowen, County Westmeath, enlisted in Mullingar. He was killed in action on 21 October 1914 at Houplines. He is buried at Houplines Communal Cemetery Extension.

Collins, Francis, Private, No 8649
Born in Langloan, Lanarkshire, resided in Coatbridge and enlisted in Glasgow. He died of wounds on 17 September 1914 at Bucy-le-Long. He has no known grave and is commemorated at La Ferté-sous-Jouarre Memorial.

Conaty, Michael, Private, No 11707
Born in Ballinagh, County Cavan, resided in Kilnaleck, County Cavan, and enlisted in Cavan. He was killed in action on 25 April 1915 at St Julien. He has no known grave and is commemorated at the Ypres (Menin Gate) Memorial.

Connolly, Charles, Private, No 11214
Born, resided and enlisted in Dublin. He died of wounds on 2 January 1915 at No 2 Clearing Hospital, Bailleul. He is buried at Bailleul Communal Cemetery and Extension.

Connor, John, Private, No 4716
Born and resided in Shankill, Belfast, and enlisted

in Lurgan, County Armagh. He was killed in action on 14 October 1914 near Houplines. He is buried at Méteren Military Cemetery.

Coogan, John, Private, No 4024
Born and resided in County Armagh, enlisted in Finner Camp, County Donegal. He was originally listed as missing and was accepted as having been killed in action on 25 April 1915 at St Julien, by the War Office on 23 August 1917. He had falsely been reported killed on 12 April 1915, and had written to his mother, advising her not to believe any reports of his death. Mrs Coogan only received this letter after official notification of his death on 25 April 1915. Distraught, and not knowing what to believe, Mrs Coogan asked Mr Trimble of the *Armagh Guardian* to investigate. He found from two other soldiers that Pte Coogan had been wounded in the ankle, and that his comrades had not been able to stop and help or carry him from the killing slopes of St Julien. Because of the letter he had written, his mother never really believed that he had been killed. He has no known grave and is commemorated at the Ypres (Menin Gate) Memorial.

Cooke, Richard, Private, No 6698
Born in Kirkham, Lancashire, resided in Whitehouse, County Antrim, and enlisted in Belfast. He was originally listed as missing and was accepted as having been killed in action on 6 November 1914, by the War Office on 18 September 1916. He has no known grave and is commemorated at the Ploegsteert Memorial.

Cope, Thomas, Private, No 7042
Born, resided and enlisted in Dublin. He was killed in action on 20 November 1914 near Armentières. He has no known grave and is commemorated at the Ploegsteert Memorial.

Copeland, John, Private, No 6484
Born in Shankill, Belfast, resided in Ballymacarret, Belfast, and enlisted in Belfast. He was killed in action on 26 April 1915 near Ypres. He has no known grave and is commemorated at the Ypres (Menin Gate) Memorial.

Cordner, Thomas, Private, No 11254
Born and resided in Portadown, County Armagh, enlisted in Armagh. He was killed in action on 9 November 1914 at Houplines. He is buried at Strand Military Cemetery.

Corrigan, Patrick, Private, No 7134
Born in Shankill, Belfast, resided and enlisted in Belfast. He was killed in action on 25 April 1915 at St Julien. He has no known grave and is commemorated at the Ypres (Menin Gate) Memorial.

Costigan, William, Private, No 11340
Born in Dublin, resided in Salford, Manchester, and enlisted in Dublin. He was originally listed as missing and was accepted as having been killed in action on 27 August 1914, by the War Office on 4 July 1916. He has no known grave and is commemorated at La Ferté-sous-Jouarre Memorial.

Courtney, James, Private, No 3471
Born and resided in Clones, County Monaghan, and enlisted in Dublin. He died of wounds on 4 December 1914 at No 10 Field Ambulance, Romarin. He is buried at Trois Arbres Cemetery.

Coyle, Edward, Private, No 11205
Born and resided in Urney, County Cavan, and enlisted in Cavan. He was killed in action on 27 August 1914 at Ligny. He is buried at Selvigny Communal Cemetery.

Crangle, John, Private, No 16377
Born in Shankill, Belfast, resided in Belfast and enlisted in Belfast. He died of wounds on 30 April 1915. He has no known grave and is commemorated at the Ypres (Menin Gate) Memorial.

Crawford, Alexander, Private, No 9971
Born and resided in Paisley, Scotland, and enlisted in Glasgow. He was killed in action on 18 October 1914 near Houplines, Armentières. He has no known grave and is commemorated at the Ploegsteert Memorial.

Crowther, William, Corporal, No 10767
Born in County Wexford, resided and enlisted in Dublin. He was killed in action on 22 October 1914 at Houplines. He is buried at Houplines Communal Cemetery Extension.

Crymble, Cecil Reginald, Lieutenant
Son of George Gordon Crymble and Agnes Templeton Crymble BA DSc of Queen's University, Belfast. He was killed in action on 20 November 1914. He has no known grave and is commemorated at the Ploegsteert Memorial.

Cully, J., Corporal, No 10353
He was originally listed as missing and was accepted as having been killed in action on 27 August 1914, by the War Office on 1 May 1916.

Daly, James, Lance Sergeant, No 9719
Born in Peshawar, India, resided and enlisted in Armagh. He was killed in action on 26 October 1914 at Houplines. He is buried at Houplines Communal Cemetery Extension.

Dempsey, James, Private, No 6450
Born in Mountmellick, Queen's County, resided in Dublin and enlisted in Naas, County Kildare. He was originally listed as missing and was accepted as having been killed in action on 25 April 1915 at St Julien, by the War Office on 27 September 1916. He has no known grave and is commemorated at the Ypres (Menin Gate) Memorial.

Dempsey, John, Private, No 11420
Born in Rathmines, Dublin, resided and enlisted in Dublin. He died on 3 November 1914. He is buried at Houplines Communal Cemetery Extension.

Dempster, Samuel, Private, No 7237
Born in Greenock, Renfrewshire, Scotland, resided and enlisted in Belfast. He was killed in action on 25 April 1915 at St Julien. He has no known grave and is commemorated at the Ypres (Menin Gate) Memorial.

Devaney, Joseph, Private, No 6324
Born, resided and enlisted in Glasgow, Scotland. He died on 21 March 1915. He is buried at Reninghelst Churchyard Extension.

Devlin, John, Private, No 8242
Born at Annaclone, County Down, resided in Rathfriland and enlisted in Newry. He was killed in action on 4 April 1915 at Douve. He has no known grave and is commemorated at the Ploegsteert Memorial. His will states, 'In the event of my death I give to Mrs Andrew Higgins, 53 Springhill Terrace, Muirkirk, Ayrshire, all my property and effects.'

Dingle, John, Private, No 9340
Born, resided and enlisted in Dublin. He was killed accidentally on 3 November 1914 at Houplines. He is buried at Houplines Communal Cemetery Extension.

Docherty, Edward, Private, No 8666
Born in Leith, resided and enlisted in Glasgow. Formerly served with the Royal Inniskilling Fusiliers, No 7264. He died of wounds on 28 April 1915 near Ypres. He has no known grave and is commemorated at the Ypres (Menin Gate) Memorial.

Donnelly, Daniel, Private, No 8752
Born and resided in Dungannon, County Tyrone, and enlisted in Belfast. Formerly served with the East Lancashire Regiment, No 8222. He was killed in action on 14 November 1914 near Armentières. He is buried at Houplines Communal Cemetery Extension.

Donnelly, James, Private, No 8374
Born and resided in Dublin, and enlisted in Naas, County Kildare. He died of wounds on 17 September 1914 at Bucy-le-Long. He has no known grave and is commemorated at La Ferté-sous-Jouarre Memorial.

Donnelly, Patrick, Private, No 11339
Born, resided and enlisted in Dublin. He was originally listed as missing and was accepted as having been killed in action on 27 August 1914, by the War Office on 15 December 1915. His will states, 'In the event of my death I give the whole of my property and effects to my mother, Ann Donnelly.' He has no known grave and is commemorated at La Ferté-sous-Jouarre Memorial.

Dowie, James, Private, No 10047
Born, resided and enlisted in Belfast. He was killed in action on 26 August 1914. The Unofficial Report of Death Form states that Lance Corporals Casey and Hagan reported that they found Pte Dowie's body on the morning of 27 August 1914. He has no known grave and is commemorated at La Ferté-sous-Jouarre Memorial.

Duffy, Thomas, Private, No 8092
Born, resided and enlisted in Arva, County Cavan. He was originally listed as missing and was accepted as having been killed in action on 27 August 1914, by the War Office on 9 June 1916. He is buried at Ham British Cemetery.

Dunlop, James, Private, No 5813
Born and resided in Ballycastle, County Antrim, and enlisted in Belfast. He was killed in action on 25 April 1915 at St Julien. He is buried at Poelcapelle British Cemetery.

Dunne, John, Private, No 11354
Born, resided and enlisted in Dublin. He was killed in action on 26 October 1914 at Houplines. He is buried at Houplines Communal Cemetery Extension.

Dunne, Martin, Private, No 11119
Born, resided and enlisted in Cavan. He was killed in action on 21 October 1914 at Houplines. He has no known grave and is commemorated at the Ploegsteert Memorial.

Dynes, Frederick, Sergeant, No 5424
Born, resided and enlisted in Lurgan, County Armagh. He was killed in action on 25 April 1915 at St Julien. He has no known grave and is commemorated at the Ypres (Menin Gate) Memorial.

Ervine, John, Private, No 5912
Born and resided in Banbridge, County Down and enlisted in Newry. He was originally listed as missing and was accepted as having been killed in action on 25 April 1915 at St Julien, by the War Office on 23 August 1917. He has no known grave and is commemorated at the Ypres (Menin Gate) Memorial.

Fanning, Francis, Private, No 8067
Born and resided in Dundalk, County Louth, and enlisted in Newry. He was originally listed as missing and was accepted as having been killed in action on 25 April 1915 at St Julien, by the War Office on 29 September 1916. He has no known grave and is commemorated at the Ypres (Menin Gate) Memorial.

Farrell, James, Private, No 9499
Born in Oldcastle, County Meath, resided and enlisted in Liverpool. He was killed in action on 25 April 1915 at St Julien. He has no known grave and is commemorated at the Ypres (Menin Gate) Memorial.

Farrell, Owen, Private, No 11505
Born, resided and enlisted in Drogheda, County Louth. He was killed in action on 25 April 1915 at St Julien. He has no known grave and is commemorated at the Ypres (Menin Gate) Memorial.

Farrell, Patrick, Private, No 2533
Born, resided and enlisted in Mount Nugent, County Cavan. He was originally listed as missing and was accepted as having been killed in action on 25 April 1915 at St Julien, by the War Office on 7 March 1918. He has no known grave and is commemorated at the Ypres (Menin Gate) Memorial.

Figes, Charles Henry, Private, No 9404
Born in Islington, north Middlesex, resided in Hackney Wick, east Middlesex, and enlisted in London. He died at home on 4 November 1914. He is buried at Leeds (Lawns Wood) Cemetery.

Flynn, William, Private, No 7189
Born in Shankill, Belfast, resided and enlisted in Belfast. He died of wounds on 20 October 1914 at Bucy-le-Long. He is buried at Cité Bonjean Military Cemetery.

Foley, James, Private, No 7709
Born, resided and enlisted in Dublin. Originally listed as missing, he was accepted as having been killed in action on 25 April 1915 at St Julien, by the War Office on 15 August 1917. He has no known grave and is commemorated at the Ypres (Menin Gate) Memorial.

Fox, James, Private, No 8704
Born and resided in Raphoe, County Donegal, and enlisted in Londonderry. Originally listed as missing and was accepted as having been killed in action on 25 April 1915 at St Julien, by the War Office on 5 October 1916. He is buried at Birr Crossroads Cemetery.

Fox, John, Private, No 5844
Born in Shankill, County Armagh, resided in Lurgan and enlisted in Portadown. He was killed in action 25 April 1915 at St Julien. His will states, 'In the event of my death, I give hold of my property and effects to Mrs D. McLarnon, Feymore, Roses Lane Ends, via Lurgan, Co Armagh.' He has no known grave and is commemorated at the Ypres (Menin Gate) Memorial.

Gannon, Patrick, Sergeant, No 10085
Born, resided and enlisted in Dublin. He was killed in action on 25 April 1915 at St Julien. His will states, 'In the event of my death, I leave all I have to my sister (property and effects) Miss Catherine Gannon, 3 Masons Yard, Fawcett St, York.' He has no known grave and is commemorated at the Ypres (Menin Gate) Memorial.

Geddis, Robert, Private, No 7887
Born and resided in Rathfriland, County Down, and enlisted in Newry. He died of wounds on 18 September 1914 at Rozieres. He is buried at Rozieres Churchyard.

Gibbens, Thomas, Private, No 9333
Born in Ashford, Kent, resided in Eastleigh, Hampshire, and enlisted in Southampton. Originally listed as missing and was accepted as having been killed in action on 25 April 1915 at St Julien, by the War Office on 8 September 1916. He has no known grave and is commemorated at the Ypres (Menin Gate) Memorial.

Godwin, Charles Blair, Sergeant No 10274
Born in Willesden NW, Middlesex, resided at Frenchay, Somerset, and enlisted in London. He attended Marlborough College. He was originally listed as missing and was accepted as having been killed in action 26 August 1914 at Haucourt, by the War Office on 6 August 1918. His grave is believed to be in Haucourt Communal Cemetery. His name is commemorated at La Ferté-sous-Jouarre Memorial.

Gorman, Peter, Private, No 7640
Born in Street, County Westmeath, resided in Hamilton, Lanarkshire, and enlisted in Mullingar. Originally listed as missing and was accepted as having been killed in action on 25 April 1915 at St Julien, by the War Office on 13 June 1916. He has no known grave and is commemorated at the Ypres (Menin Gate) Memorial.

Graham, Albert, Private, No 8692
Born and resided in Shankill, County Armagh, and enlisted in Lurgan. Originally listed as missing and was accepted as having been killed in action on 25 April 1915 at St Julien, by the War Office on 18 September 1916. He has no known grave and is commemorated at the Ypres (Menin Gate) Memorial.

Graham, David, Private, No 6809
Born and resided in Greencastle, County Antrim, and enlisted in Belfast. He was killed in action on 21 October 1914 at Houplines. He has no known grave and is commemorated at the Ploegsteert Memorial.

Gray, Bernard, Private, No 3299
Born, resided and enlisted in Cavan into the 4th Battalion (Special Reserve) Royal Irish Fusiliers. He was killed in action on 12 April 1915 at Armentières. He has no known grave and is commemorated at the Ploegsteert Memorial.

Gray, William, Private, No 7541
Born and resided in Dundalk, County Louth, and enlisted in Warrington, Lancashire. Originally listed as missing and was accepted as having been killed in action on 25 April 1915 at St Julien, by the War Office on 7 November 1916. He is buried at Bedford House Cemetery.

Greenaway, Francis, Private, No 6119
Born and resided in Portadown and enlisted in Armagh. He died of wounds received at St Julien, on 28 April 1915 at No 13 General Hospital, Boulogne. He is buried at Boulogne Eastern Cemetery.

Greenwood, George, Private, No 9323
Born and resided in Bromley, Kent, and enlisted at Woolwich. He was killed in action on 25 April 1915 at St Julien. He has no known grave and is commemorated at the Ypres (Menin Gate) Memorial.

Gribben, Thomas, Private, No 8228
Born in Downpatrick, County Down, resided in Killyleagh, County Down, and enlisted at Downpatrick. Originally listed as missing and was accepted as having been killed in action on 25 April 1915 at St Julien, by the War Office on 17 August 1917. He has no known grave and is commemorated at the Ypres (Menin Gate) Memorial.

Haddock, Samuel, Private, No 11309
Born at Shankill, County Armagh, resided in Lurgan and enlisted in Portadown. He died of wounds on 27 January 1915 at No 13 Stationary Hospital, Boulogne. He is buried at Boulogne Eastern Cemetery.

Hampson, John, Private, No 8483
Born and resided in Killoe, County Longford, and enlisted at Armagh. He died of wounds on 1 November 1914 at No 2 Clearing Hospital, Bailleul. He is buried at Bailleul Communal Cemetery and Extension.

Hanvey, William, Private, No 11158
Born and resided in Portadown, and enlisted at Armagh. He died of wounds on 8 November 1914 at No 10 Field Ambulance. He is buried at Trois Arbres Cemetery.

Hayden, Christopher, Private, No 9013
Born in Longford, resided in Birmingham and enlisted in Longford. He died on 5 April 1915 as a result of a self-inflicted gunshot wound at

Armentières. His will states, 'In the event of my death I give the whole of my property and effects to my sister, Mary Fred Davis, No 2 Hettie Place, Prescott St, Brookfields, Birmingham.' He is buried at Cité Bonjean Military Cemetery.

Healy, William, Private, No 7609
Born, resided and enlisted in Dublin. He was killed in action on 25 April 1915 at St Julien. He has no known grave and is commemorated at the Ypres (Menin Gate) Memorial.

Henson, Henry Frederick, Private, No 10379
Born at St Peter's, Middlesex, resided in Battersea, Surrey, and enlisted at Aldershot. He was killed in action on 25 April 1915 at St Julien. He is buried at Bedford House Cemetery.

Hetherington, Richard, Corporal, No 8135
Born and resided at Mountrath, Queen's County, enlisted at Maryborough, Queen's County. He was killed in action on 8 September 1914 near Bucy-le-Long. He has no known grave and is commemorated at La Ferté-sous-Jouarre Memorial.

Hill, Denis, Private, No 7299
Born in Dublin, resided in Saltcoats, Ayrshire, and enlisted in Dublin. Originally listed as missing and was accepted as having been killed in action on 25 April 1915 at St Julien, by the War Office on 5 October 1916. He has no known grave and is commemorated at the Ypres (Menin Gate) Memorial.

Holden, Joseph, Private, No 8306
Born in Strabane, County Tyrone, resided in Glasgow, and enlisted in Londonderry. He died of wounds on 25 April 1915 at No 2 Clearing Hospital, Bailleul. He is buried at Poperinghe Old Military Cemetery.

Humphreys, William, Private, No 5176
Born at Shankill, County Armagh, resided in Belfast, and enlisted at Portadown. He was killed in action on 25 April 1915 at St Julien. His will states, 'In the event of my death, I give the whole of my property and effects to my mother, Rachel Humphreys, 63 Ottawa St, Belfast.' He has no known grave and is commemorated at the Ypres (Menin Gate) Memorial.

Hyde, James, Private, No 11229
Born and resided in Clones, County Monaghan, and enlisted in Belfast. He was killed in action on 25 April 1915 at St Julien. His will states, 'In the event of my death I give the whole of my property and effects to my mother, Mrs Hyde, 86 Hunter St, off Linfield Rd, Belfast.' He has no known grave and is commemorated at the Ypres (Menin Gate) Memorial.

Hylands, Thomas, Private, No 4760
Born at Donaghcloney, County Down, resided in Lurgan, and enlisted at Finner Camp, County Donegal. He served with the 3rd (Special Reserve) Battalion Royal Irish Fusiliers and was mobilised into the 1st Bn when the Great War started. He was killed in action on 22 December 1914 at Ploegsteert near Armentières. He has no known grave and is commemorated at the Ploegsteert Memorial.

Jackson, John, Private, No 5231
Born and resided in Shankill, County Armagh, and enlisted at Lurgan into the 3rd (Special Reserve) Battalion Royal Irish Fusiliers. He was killed in action on 12 April 1915. He has no known grave and is commemorated at the Ploegsteert Memorial.

Jebb, John, Private, No 8786
Born in Monaghan, County Monaghan, resided in Glasgow, and enlisted at Monaghan. He was killed in action on 18 September 1914 near Bucy-le-Long. He has no known grave and is commemorated at La Ferté-sous-Jouarre Memorial.

Johnston, Robert, Private, No 8773
Born, resided and enlisted in Carlisle, Cumberland. He was killed in action on 21 October 1914 at Houplines. He is buried at Houplines Communal Cemetery Extension.

Johnston, Samuel, Private, No 11201
Born and resided in Carrickfergus, County Antrim, and enlisted in Lurgan, County Armagh. He died at home on 30 November 1914. He is buried at Portsdown (Christchurch) Military Cemetery, Hampshire.

Jones, David Carson, Sergeant, No 9560, DCM
Born, resided and enlisted at Cloverhill, County Cavan. He died of wounds on 20 October 1914 near Armentières. He is buried at Cité Bonjean Military Cemetery.

Kane, Henry, Private, No 8361
Born and resided in Belfast, and enlisted in Armagh. He died of wounds on 21 December 1914

at British Hospital Boulogne. He is buried at Wimereux Communal Cemetery.

Kavanagh, Alfred, Private, No 11069

Born and resided in Portarlington, Queen's County, enlisted at Monaghan. He was killed in action on 21 October 1914 at Houplines. He is buried at Houplines Communal Cemetery Extension.

Kavanagh, Joseph, Private, No 6696

Born in Dublin, resided in Govanhill, Lanarkshire, and enlisted in Dublin. He was killed in action on 17 November 1914 near Armentières. He is buried at Houplines Communal Cemetery Extension.

Keinzley, James, Private, No 3726

Born, resided and enlisted in Portadown. He died at home on 20 March 1915. He is buried at Drumcree Roman Catholic Churchyard.

Kelly, Edward, Private, No 7617

Born, resided and enlisted at Newtownmount-kennedy, County Wicklow. He died of wounds on 26 October 1914 at No 11 Field Ambulance, Armentières. He is buried at Cité Bonjean Military Cemetery.

Kelly, James Patrick, Sergeant, No 8173

Born, resided and enlisted at Armagh. He died of wounds on 31 March 1915. He is buried at Boulogne Eastern Cemetery.

Kelly, Joseph, Private, No 6625

Born at Navan, County Meath, resided at Wilkinstown, County Meath, and enlisted at Drogheda. He died of wounds on 18 October 1914 at No 11 Field Ambulance, Armentières. He is buried at Cité Bonjean Military Cemetery.

Kelly, Patrick, Private, No 6303

Born and resided in Bray, County Wicklow, and enlisted in Monkstown, County Dublin. He was killed in action 8 November 1914 at Houplines. He is buried at Strand Military Cemetery.

Keogh, John, Private, No 8553

Born, resided and enlisted in Dublin. He died of wounds on 30 November 1914 at No 10 Field Ambulance at Romarin. He is buried at Trois Arbres Cemetery.

Kiernan, Edward, private, 7626

Born, resided and enlisted in Mullingar, County Westmeath. Originally listed as missing and was accepted as having been killed in action on 25 April 1915 at St Julien, by the War Office on 18 September 1916. He has no known grave and is commemorated at the Ypres (Menin Gate) Memorial.

Larkin, John, Private, No 6158

Born, resided and enlisted in Dundalk, County Louth. He was killed in action on 25 April 1915 at St Julien. He has no known grave and is commemorated at the Ypres (Menin Gate) Memorial.

Lavery, Owen, Private, No 5087

Born, resided and enlisted in Newry, County Down. Originally listed as missing and was accepted as having been killed in action on 25 April 1915 at St Julien, by the War Office on 11 January 1917. He has no known grave and is commemorated at the Ypres (Menin Gate) Memorial.

Lee, Michael, Private, No 11446

Born, resided and enlisted in Dublin. He was killed in action on 26 August 1914. He is buried at Honnechy British Cemetery.

Livingstone, James, Private, No 11317

Born and resided in Shankill, County Armagh, and enlisted at Lurgan. He was killed in action on 26 October 1914 at Houplines. He is buried at Houplines Communal Cemetery Extension.

Lynden-Bell, Donald Perceval, Lieutenant

The son of Col Charles Perceval Lynden-Bell JP of Fairlawn House, Tadley, Basingstoke, Hampshire. He joined the Battalion on 26 December 1914, and was aged 19 when he was killed in action on 25 April 1915 at St Julien. He is buried at New Irish Farm Cemetery.

Lyons, Leonard Bernard, Sergeant No 10271

Born at Maidstone, Kent, resided at Battersea SW, Surrey, and enlisted at Leicester. Formerly served with Royal Fusiliers, No 6305. He died of wounds on 19 September 1914 at Rozieres. He is buried at Rozieres Churchyard.

Lyons, Michael, Private, No 7985

Born and resided in Maryborough, Queen's County, and enlisted at Cootehill, County Cavan. He died of wounds on 28 April 1914 at No 8 Casualty Clearing Station. He is buried at Bailleul Communal Cemetery and Extension.

Lyster, John, Private, No 8265

Born, resided and enlisted in Kingstown, County Dublin. He was killed in action on 18 September

1914 at Bucy-le-Long. He is buried at Vauxbuin French National Cemetery.

Magee, Edward, Private, No 8507
Born, resided and enlisted in Belfast. He was originally listed as missing and was accepted as having been killed in action on 27 August 1914, by the War Office on 15 December 1915. He is buried at Bantouzelle Communal Cemetery.

Magee, Thomas, Private, No 7403
Born and resided in Dublin, and enlisted in Leeds. He was killed in action on 28 October 1914 at Houplines. He is buried at Houplines Communal Cemetery Extension.

Magill, John, Private, No 5260
Born Shankill, County Armagh, resided Lurgan, County Armagh, and enlisted at Portadown, County Armagh. He died of wounds on 27 April 1915 at No 2 Casualty Clearing Hospital. His will states, 'In the event of my death I leave all of my property and effects to my sister, Miss Ellen Jane Magill, 50 North St, Lurgan.' He is buried at Bailleul Communal Cemetery and Extension.

Magill, William, Private, No 8391
Born, resided and enlisted in Belfast. He was killed in action on 21 November 1914 at Ploegsteert. He has no known grave and is commemorated at the Ploegsteert Memorial.

Mahaffey, Joseph, Private, No 6612
Born and resided at Shankill, County Armagh, and enlisted at Lurgan. He was killed in action on 21 November 1914 near Armentières. He has no known grave and is commemorated at the Ploegsteert Memorial.

Malcolm, William, Private, No 8204
Born and resided in Holywood, County Down, enlisted in Belfast. Originally listed as missing and was accepted as having been killed in action on 25 April 1915 at St Julien, by the War Office on 5 October 1916. He has no known grave and is commemorated at the Ypres (Menin Gate) Memorial.

Malcolmson, William, Private, No 4142
Born and resided in Portadown, County Armagh, and enlisted at Finner Camp, County Donegal. He was killed in action on 25 April 1915 at St Julien. He has no known grave and is commemorated at the Ypres (Menin Gate) Memorial.

Mallon, Joseph, Private, No 9207
Born and resided in Belfast, enlisted at Ballykinlar, County Down. He died of wounds on 27 September 1914 at British Herbert Hospital, Paris. He is buried at Levallois-perret Communal Cemetery.

Manning, Percy, Private, No 11248
Born and resided in Waterford, and enlisted at Dublin. He died of wounds on 8 November 1914 at No 2 Clearing Hospital, Ballieul. He is buried at Bailleul Communal Cemetery and Extension.

Mercer, James, Private, No 9279
Born at Holmwood, Surrey, resided at Fulham, and enlisted in London. He was originally listed as missing and was accepted as having been killed in action on 27 August 1914 by the War Office on 15 December 1915. He has no known grave and is commemorated at La Ferté-sous-Jouarre Memorial.

Millar, Arthur James, Captain
Son of James and Isabella Millar of 87 Eglantine Avenue, Belfast. He was aged 24 when he was killed in action on 25 April 1915 at St Julien. He has no known grave and is commemorated at the Ypres (Menin Gate) Memorial.

Mills, John, Private, No 8527
Born and resided in Portadown, and enlisted in Lurgan. He was killed in action on 25 April 1915 at St Julien. He has no known grave and is commemorated at the Ypres (Menin Gate) Memorial.

Moore, Robert James, Private, No 8403
Born and resided in Armagh, and enlisted at Lurgan. He was killed in action on 29 November 1914 at Nieppe. He has no known grave and is commemorated at the Ploegsteert Memorial.

Moran, John, Lance Corporal, No 11005
Born, resided and enlisted at Dublin. He was killed in action on 22 February 1915 at Douve near Armentières. He has no known grave and is commemorated at the Ploegsteert Memorial.

Morrow, James Stewart, Private, No 7683
Born and resided at Knockbride, County Cavan, enlisted at Cootehill, County Cavan. He was killed in action on 18 October 1914 near Houplines. He is buried at Houplines Communal Cemetery Extension.

Morrow, Robert, Private, No 10531, VC
Born at Carland, County Tyrone, resided at New

Mills, County Tyrone and enlisted at Dungannon. He died of wounds received at the Battle of St Julien on 26 April 1915. He is buried at White House Cemetery.

Mulholland, John, Private, No 5393
Born and resided in Dundalk, and enlisted at Newry. Originally listed as missing and was accepted as having been killed in action on 25 April 1915 at St Julien, by the War Office on 23 August 1917. He has no known grave and is commemorated at the Ypres (Menin Gate) Memorial.

Mullany, D. (served as St Ruth, R.), Private, No 11203 or 10203
He was killed in action on 25 April 1915 at St Julien.

Mullen Patrick, Private, No 11436
Born, resided and enlisted in Dublin. He was killed in action on 26 August 1914. He has no known grave and is commemorated at La Ferté-sous-Jouarre Memorial.

Munro, James, Private, No 10935
Born and resided in Coatbridge, Lanarkshire, and enlisted in Glasgow. He was originally listed as missing and was accepted as having been killed in action on 26 August 1914, by the War Office on 3 March 1916. He has no known grave and is commemorated at La Ferté-sous-Jouarre Memorial.

Murphy, James Joseph, Private, No 11210
Born and resided in Glasgow, and enlisted in London. He was killed in action on 12 April 1915 at Armentières. He has no known grave and is commemorated at the Ploegsteert Memorial.

Murphy, Patrick, Private, No 8942
Born, resided and enlisted in Dublin. He died of chronic bronchitis and emphysema on 6 January 1915 at No 2 Clearing Hospital, Bailleul. He is buried at Bailleul Communal Cemetery and Extension.

Murray, Andrew, Private, No 5122
Born at Shankill, County Armagh, resided in Lurgan, and enlisted in Portadown. Originally listed as missing and was accepted as having been killed in action on 25 April 1915 at St Julien, by the War Office on 29 September 1916. He has no known grave and is commemorated at the Ypres (Menin Gate) Memorial.

Murray, Thomas, Sergeant, No 10491
Born, resided and enlisted in Dublin. He was killed in action on 25 April 1915 at St Julien. He has no known grave and is commemorated at the Ypres (Menin Gate) Memorial.

Murtagh, Thomas, Private, No 3295
Born, resided and enlisted in Ballinagh, County Cavan. Originally listed as missing and was accepted as having been killed in action on 25 April 1915 at St Julien, by the War Office on 5 October 1916. He has no known grave and is commemorated at the Ypres (Menin Gate) Memorial.

McCann, Thomas John, Private, No 11495
Born, resided and enlisted in Portadown. He died of wounds on 21 October 1914. He is buried at Cité Bonjean Military Cemetery.

McCartney, John, Private, No 7856
Born in Dublin, resided in Laurencetown, County Down, and enlisted in Hamilton, Lanarkshire. He was killed in action on 25 April 1915 at St Julien. He has no known grave and is commemorated at the Ypres (Menin Gate) Memorial.

McClarnan (or McClarnon), William, Private, No 11295
Born, resided and enlisted in Preston, Lancashire. Formerly served with Dragoons of the Line, No 7939. Originally listed as missing and was accepted as having been killed in action on 25 April 1915 at St Julien, by the War Office on 23 August 1917. He has no known grave and is commemorated at the Ypres (Menin Gate) Memorial.

McConville, Charles Vincent, Private, No 11215
Born and resided in Shankill, County Armagh, and enlisted at Lurgan. He was originally listed as missing and was accepted as having been killed in action on 26 August 1914, by the War Office on 9 June 1916. He has no known grave and is commemorated at La Ferté-sous-Jouarre Memorial.

McConville, Matthew, Private, No 5726
Born at Shankill, County Armagh, resided in Belfast, and enlisted at Lurgan. He was killed in action on 28 April 1915. His will states, 'In the event of my death I give the whole of my property and effects to my grandmother, Maria Shanks, Lower North St, Lurgan.' He has no known grave and is commemorated at the Ypres (Menin Gate) Memorial.

McCormack, Edward, Private, No 5788
Born and resided in Cavan, and enlisted in Armagh. Originally listed as missing and was accepted as having been killed in action on 25 April 1915 at St Julien, by the War Office on 29 September 1916. He has no known grave and is commemorated at the Ypres (Menin Gate) Memorial.

McCourt, Michael, Private, No 5904
Born at Coatbridge, Lanarkshire, resided at Camlough, County Armagh, and enlisted in Newry. He was killed in action on 25 April 1915 at St Julien. He has no known grave and is commemorated at the Ypres (Menin Gate) Memorial.

McDonald, John, Private, No 8467
Born at Lisnaskea, County Fermanagh, resided in Gilford, and enlisted in Armagh. He was killed in action on 14 November 1914 near Armentières. He is buried at Houplines Communal Cemetery Extension.

McDowell, Samuel, Private, No 4329
Born in Armagh, resided in Lurgan, and enlisted at Finner Camp, County Donegal. He was killed in action on 25 April 1915 at St Julien. His will states, 'In the event of my death, I give the whole of my property and effects to Mrs Annie McDowell, 6 Wilson's Row, Avenue Road, Lurgan.' He has no known grave and is commemorated at the Ypres (Menin Gate) Memorial.

McElroy, Peter, Private, No 5430
Born, resided and enlisted in Newry, County Down. He served with the 3rd (Special Reserve) Battalion Royal Irish Fusiliers and was mobilised into the 1st Battalion when the Great War started. He died of wounds on 13 April 1915 at No 2 Clearing Hospital, Bailleul. He is buried at Bailleul Communal Cemetery and Extension.

McEvoy, Gordon, Sergeant, No 9354
Born at St Giles, Middlesex, and enlisted in London. He was killed in action on 21 October 1914 at Houplines. He is buried at Houplines Communal Cemetery Extension.

McGeown, Francis, Private, No 5971
Born and resided at Shankill, County Armagh, and enlisted in Lurgan. Originally listed as missing and was accepted as having been killed in action on 25 April 1915 at St Julien, by the War Office on 29 September 1916. He has no known grave and is commemorated at the Ypres (Menin Gate) Memorial.

McGlone, John, Private, No 6741
Born, resided and enlisted in Glasgow. He was killed in action on 10 November 1914 at Houplines. He is buried at Strand Military Cemetery.

McGrath, John, Private, 11237
Born and resided in Seapatrick, County Down, and enlisted in Portadown, County Armagh. He died of wounds on 15 October 1914 at Hazebrouck. He is buried at Hazebrouck Communal Cemetery.

McGrath, Joseph, Private, No 9730
Born and resided in Enniskillen, County Fermanagh, and enlisted at Dublin. He was killed in action on 26 August 1914 at Haucourt. He has no known grave and is commemorated at La Ferté-sous-Jouarre Memorial.

McKenna, Francis, Private, No 11038
Born and resided in Dundalk, and enlisted in Cavan. He died of wounds on 21 October 1914 at No 3 Ambulance Train from Armentières to Base. He has no known grave and is commemorated at the Ploegsteert Memorial.

McKeown, Charles, Private, No 11142
Born, resided and enlisted in Portadown, County Armagh. Originally listed as missing and was accepted as having been killed in action on 25 April 1915 at St Julien, by the War Office on 5 October 1916. He has no known grave and is commemorated at the Ypres (Menin Gate) Memorial.

McKevitt, James, Private, No 8279
Born, resided and enlisted in Newry, County Down. He died of wounds on 26 April 1915 at No 84 Field Ambulance. His will states, 'In the event of my death I give to my wife all the property I have. Witnessed by James Duffy and James Murray.' He is buried at Poperinghe Old Military Cemetery.

McMurray, William Thomas, Private, No 10615
Born, resided and enlisted in Clones, County Monaghan. He was killed in action on 25 April 1915 at St Julien. His will states, 'All to mother.' He is buried at Seaforth Cemetery.

McNally, Peter, Private, No 10462
Born, resided and enlisted at Cootehill, County

Cavan. He was killed in action on 27 August 1914. He is buried at Bantouzelle Communal Cemetery.

McShane, Robert, Private, No 8751
Born and resided at Dungannon, County Tyrone, and enlisted at Armagh. He was killed in action on 27 August 1914 at Haucourt. He is buried at Esnes Communal Cemetery.

McStravick, John, Private, No 11438
Born and resided in Shankill, County Armagh, and enlisted at Lurgan. He was killed in action on 25 April 1915 at St Julien. He has no known grave and is commemorated at the Ypres (Menin Gate) Memorial.

Neill, George, Private, No 10772
Born, resided and enlisted in Portadown, County Armagh. Originally listed as missing and was accepted as having been killed in action on 27 August 1914, by the War Office on 15 December 1915. He is buried at Honnechy British Cemetery.

Nevin, Patrick, Private, No 3141
Born and resided in Limerick, and enlisted in Dublin. Originally listed as missing and was accepted as having been killed in action on 25 April 1915 at St Julien, by the War Office on 18 September 1916. He has no known grave and is commemorated at the Ypres (Menin Gate) Memorial.

Nolan, Michael, Drummer, No 11169
Born, resided and enlisted in Dublin. He was killed in action on 18 October 1914 at Bailleul. He is buried at Bailleul Communal Cemetery and Extension.

O'Brien, Joseph, Private, No 8980
Born, resided and enlisted at Charleville, County Cork. Originally listed as missing and was accepted as having been killed in action on 26 August 1914, by the War Office on 15 February 1916. He has no known grave and is commemorated at La Ferté-sous-Jouarre Memorial.

O'Hara, Robert James, Private, No 8161
Born, resided and enlisted in Belfast. He died of pneumonia on 28 March 1915 at No 4 General Hospital, Versailles. His will states, 'In the event of my death, I give all my money to my wife, after my debts are paid, Mrs E. O'Hara, Urekena St, Belfast.' He is buried at Les Gonards Cemetery, Versailles.

O'Neill, Alfred, Private, No 8011
Born and resided in Whitehouse, County Antrim, and enlisted at Belfast. He was killed in action on 21 October 1914 at Houplines. He has no known grave and is commemorated at the Ploegsteert Memorial.

O'Rourke, J., Private, No 10502
He was killed in action on 25 April 1915 at St Julien.

O'Sullivan, W., Private, No 10233
He was originally listed as missing and was accepted as having been killed in action on 27 August 1914, by the War Office on 29 March 1916.

Parks, Robert, Private, No 9990
Born and resided in Shankill, County Armagh, and enlisted in Portadown, County Armagh. Originally listed as missing and was accepted as having been killed in action on 26 August 1914, by the War Office on 24 July 1916. He is buried at Honnechy British Cemetery.

Patterson, Samuel, Private, No 8229
Born in Saintfield, County Down, resided at Boardmills, County Down, and enlisted at Belfast. He was killed in action on 25 April 1915 at St Julien. He has no known grave and is commemorated at the Ypres (Menin Gate) Memorial.

Penrose, Edward John McNeill, Captain
The son of the Reverend John T. and Annie C. L. Penrose of 'Tullaghquin', Church Road, Wimbledon, London. He embarked with the Battalion on 23 August 1914. He was only 27 years old when he was killed in action on 25 April 1915. In December 1919 his father received from a German professor at Aachen some papers belonging to his son, which he, the professor, said had been found in a dugout on the Hanebeek on 25 April 1915. He has no known grave and is commemorated on the Ypres (Menin Gate) Memorial.

Phibbs, W. G. B., Major
He died of pneumonia at home on 8 November 1914. Buried at Llangefni Cemetery, Anglesey.

Pollard, Thomas, Private, No 6733
Born and resided in Randalstown, County Antrim, and enlisted at Belfast. He was killed in action on 18 October 1914 near Houplines. He has no known

grave and is commemorated at the Ploegsteert Memorial.

Pratt, Thomas, Private, No 7725
Born and resided at Clones, County Monaghan, and enlisted at Belfast. Originally listed as missing and was accepted as having been killed in action on 26 August 1914, by the War Office on 20 June 1916. His will states, 'In the event of my death I give to my wife Mrs N. Pratt all my money due after my debts are paid, this will be sent to 36 Benwell St, Belfast.' He has no known grave and is commemorated at La Ferté-sous-Jouarre Memorial.

Quinn, William, Private, No 7777
Born and resided in Shankill, County Armagh, and enlisted at Lurgan. He died of wounds received at St Julien on 27 April 1915, and his body was transferred from No 9 Ambulance Train to No 10 Stationary Hospital, St Omer. He is buried at Longuenesse (St Omer) Souvenir Cemetery.

Radmilovic, Paul, Sergeant, No 9293
Born in Cardiff, resided in Folkestone, Kent, and enlisted at Cardiff. He was killed in action on 25 April 1915 at St Julien. He is buried at Poelcapelle British Cemetery.

Rafferty, John, Private, No 11308
Born and resided in Maynooth, County Kildare, enlisted at Dublin. He died of wounds on 29 November 1914 at No 2 Clearing Hospital, Bailleul. He is buried at Bailleul Communal Cemetery and Extension.

Ranaghan, Patrick, Private, No 9058
Born in Strathblane, Stirling, resided Maryhill, Glasgow, and enlisted at Glasgow. He was killed in action on 25 April 1915 at St Julien. He has no known grave and is commemorated at the Ypres (Menin Gate) Memorial.

Reaney, Edward Thomas, Private, No 9467
Born and resided in Shankill, Belfast, enlisted at Armagh. Originally listed as missing and was accepted as having been killed in action on 25 April 1915 at St Julien, by the War Office on 29 September 1916. He has no known grave and is commemorated at the Ypres (Menin Gate) Memorial.

Regan, William, Private, No 8981
Born, resided and enlisted at Charleville, County Cork. He was killed in action on 26 August 1914. He has no known grave and is commemorated at La Ferté-sous-Jouarre Memorial.

Reilly, George Bernard, Private, No 8088
Born in Granard, County Longford, resided in Carrick on Shannon, County Leitrim, and enlisted at Cavan. Originally listed as missing and was accepted as having been killed in action on 15 October 1914, by the War Office on 12 August 1916. He has no known grave and is commemorated at the Ploegsteert Memorial.

Russell, W., Private, No 11352
Originally listed as missing, he was accepted as having been killed in action on 27 August 1914, by the War Office on 1 September 1916.

Ryan, Richard, Private, No 9330
Born in Bermondsey, Surrey, resided at Streatham Hill, Surrey, and enlisted at London. Originally listed as missing and was accepted as having been killed in action on 25 April 1915 at St Julien, by the War Office on 5 October 1916. He has no known grave and is commemorated at the Ypres (Menin Gate) Memorial.

Samuels, Arthur Molesworth, Second Lieutenant
Son of the late Lt Col William Frederick Samuels AMS and Althea Samuels of Kingstown, County Dublin. He was aged 25 when he was killed in action on 13 October 1914. He is buried at Méteren Military Cemetery.

Scott (alias Unkles), Robert, Sergeant, No 9605
Born and resided at Skreen, County Sligo, and enlisted at Glasgow. He died of wounds on 26 October 1915 at No 11 Field Ambulance, Armentières. He is buried at Cité Bonjean Military Cemetery.

Scott, William, Private, No 9642
Born and resided in Hammersmith W, Middlesex, and enlisted at London. He was killed in action on 27 August 1914. He is buried at Esnes Communal Cemetery.

Sharp, John, Private, No 6927
Born and resided at Rutherglen, Lanarkshire, and enlisted at Glasgow. He was killed in action on 25 April 1915 at St Julien. He has no known grave and is commemorated at the Ypres (Menin Gate) Memorial.

Sheil, Andrew, Lance Corporal, No 9180
Born, resided and enlisted in Dublin. He was killed

in action on 18 October 1914 near Houplines. He is buried at Houplines Communal Cemetery Extension.

Shields, Humphrey, Private, No 8562
Born at Paisley, Renfrewshire, resided at Coatbridge, Lanarkshire, and enlisted at Glasgow. He was killed in action on 25 April 1915 at St Julien. He has no known grave and is commemorated at the Ypres (Menin Gate) Memorial.

Shiveral, Samuel, Private, No 9115
Born at Keady, County Armagh, resided at Sittingbourne, Kent, and enlisted at Hamilton, Lanarkshire. He was killed in action on 14 October 1914 near Houplines. He is buried at Méteren Military Cemetery.

Small, William Francis, Private, No 11387
Born in Limerick, resided in Buttevant, County Cork, and enlisted in Mallow, County Cork. He was killed in action on 25 April 1915 at St Julien. He has no known grave and is commemorated at the Ypres (Menin Gate) Memorial.

Smith, Jesse, Private, No 7571
Born, resided and enlisted in Northampton. He was killed in action on 25 October 1914 at Houplines. He is buried at Houplines Communal Cemetery Extension.

Sproule, Joseph, Company Sergeant Major, No 7917
Born in Kesh, County Fermanagh, resided in Clones, County Monaghan, and enlisted in Monaghan. He was killed in action on 8 December 1914 at Douve. He has no known grave and is commemorated at the Ploegsteert Memorial.

Steele, Thomas William, Private, No 11376
Born, resided and enlisted in Cookstown, County Tyrone. Formerly served with the Royal Inniskilling Fusiliers, No 11376. He was killed in action on 16 September 1914 near Bucy-le-Long. He has no known grave and is commemorated at the La Ferté-sous-Jouarre Memorial.

Sullivan, John, Private, No 11172
Born and resided in Cavan, and enlisted at Glasgow. He died of wounds on 20 October 1914 at No 1 Ambulance Train. He is buried at Hazebrouck Communal Cemetery.

Sullivan, Joseph, Private, No 11204
Born, resided and enlisted in Cavan. His Army Death Form is annotated as follows: 'Reported by OC Unit 26 August 1914. Source of information on which this report is based – List of killed In Action or Died of Wounds at Clary, Nord, on 27 August 1914, from American Ambassador to Foreign Office. He was killed in action probably on 27 August 1914 at Clary, Nord.' He is buried at Honnechy British Cemetery.

Summerville, William, Private, No 11402
Born, resided and enlisted at Portadown. He died of wounds on 17 September 1914 at Bucy-le-Long. He has no known grave and is commemorated at La Ferté-sous-Jouarre Memorial.

Taylor, Stephen, Private, No 9361
Born and resided in Battersea, and enlisted at London. He was killed in action on 9 November 1914 at Houplines. He is buried at Strand Military Cemetery.

Tedford, Charles, Private, No 7354
Born in Portadown, resided in Coatbridge, Lanarkshire, and enlisted at Portadown. He was killed in action on 25 April 1915 at St Julien. He has no known grave and is commemorated at the Ypres (Menin Gate) Memorial.

Thomas, Elwin, Private, No 11082
Born, resided and enlisted in Dublin. He was killed in action on 26 October 1914 at Houplines. He is buried at Houplines Communal Cemetery Extension.

Todd, William Francis, Private, No 7365
Born and resided in Shankill, Belfast, and enlisted at Portadown, County Armagh. He was killed in action on 22 October 1914 at Houplines. He is buried at Houplines Communal Cemetery Extension.

Toman, John, Private, No 5180
Born in Lurgan, resided in Portadown, and enlisted at Lurgan. Originally listed as missing, and was accepted as having been killed in action on 25 April 1915 at St Julien, by the War Office on 29 September 1916. He has no known grave and is commemorated at the Ypres (Menin Gate) Memorial.

Wakefield, Roger Owen Birbeck, Lieutenant
He died of wounds on 28 August 1914 at Coubrai. He is buried at Caudry Old Communal Cemetery.

Walmsley, William, Private, No 5787
Born and resided in Dundalk, County Louth, and enlisted at Armagh. He was killed in action on 25 April 1915 at St Julien. He has no known grave and is commemorated at the Ypres (Menin Gate) Memorial.

Walsh, John, Private, No 7106
Born, resided and enlisted at Sligo. He died of wounds on 27 October 1914 at No 11 Field Ambulance. He is buried at Cité Bonjean Military Cemetery.

Ward, William, Private, No 9373
Born and resided in Southwark, Surrey, and enlisted at Stratford E, Essex. He died of wounds on 19 September 1914 at Neuilly. He is buried at Neuilly-sur-Seine New Communal Cemetery.

Watson, William, Private, No 4734
Born in Armagh, resided in Lurgan, and enlisted at Finner Camp, County Donegal. He served with the 3rd (Special Reserve) Battalion Royal Irish Fusiliers and was mobilised into the 1st Bn when the Great War started. He was killed in action on 27 November 1914 near Armentières. He has no known grave and is commemorated at the Ploegsteert Memorial.

Watson, William, Private, No 11529
Born in Holywood, County Down, resided in Saintfield, County Down, and enlisted at Cavan. He was killed in action on 12 April 1915. He has no known grave and is commemorated at the Ploegsteert Memorial.

Whelehan, Christopher, Private, No 11496
Born, resided and enlisted at Mullingar, County Westmeath. Formerly served with the 5th Battalion Leinster Regiment, No 4565. He was killed in action on 13 April 1915. He has no known grave and is commemorated at the Ploegsteert Memorial.

Whelton, John, Private, No 9652
Born, resided and enlisted at Dunmanway, County Cork. He was killed in action on 3 November 1914. He has no known grave and is commemorated at the Ploegsteert Memorial.

Whyte, Charles, Private, No 8350
Born, resided and enlisted at Dublin. He was killed in action on 26 October 1914 at Houplines. He is buried at Houplines Communal Cemetery Extension.

Woodhouse, Thomas, Private, No 8355
Born and resided in Portadown, and enlisted at Armagh. He was killed in action on 21 October 1914 at Houplines. He is buried at Houplines Communal Cemetery Extension.

Woods, Samuel James, Private, No 11355
Born, resided and enlisted at Portadown. He was killed in action on 25 April 1915 at St Julien. He has no known grave and is commemorated at the Ypres (Menin Gate) Memorial.

Woods, William John, Private, No 7445
Born in Portadown, resided in Cowcaddens, Glasgow, and enlisted at Portadown. He was killed in action on 14 November 1914 near Armentières. He is buried at Houplines Communal Cemetery Extension.

Wright, James, Corporal, No 9631
Born at Stratford E, Essex, resided in Deptford, Kent, and enlisted at New Kent Road SE, Surrey. Originally listed as missing and was accepted as having been killed in action on 25 April 1915 at St Julien by the War Office on 5 October 1916. He has no known grave and is commemorated at the Ypres (Menin Gate) Memorial.

Wright, John, Private, No 7064
Real name was Edward Shaw. Born in Belfast, resided in Enniskillen, and enlisted at Belfast. The son of George and Margaret Shaw and the husband of Annie Shaw of 9 New Row, Enniskillen. He was aged 29 when he was killed in action on 25 April 1915 at St Julien. He has no known grave and is commemorated at the Ypres (Menin Gate) Memorial.

Yeates, John, Private, No 11455
Born, resided and enlisted at Dublin. He was killed in action on 25 April 1915 at St Julien. He is buried at Poelcapelle British Cemetery.

Appendix 1
Biography of Sgt Hugh Alexander Wilson

The son of Samuel and Mary Wilson, Hugh was born in the Presbyterian parish of Knocknagor near Gilford, Co Down, on 30 April 1885. He had a brother, Samuel, and two sisters, Marion and Lily. By the time he was 16 years old the Wilson family had moved to Manchester. Hugh followed the family tradition and joined his father's regiment, the Manchesters, on 26 August 1901, when he was just 16 years and three months old, a Boy soldier. He was just 5 feet tall with blue eyes and auburn hair, and had a heart tattooed on his forearm.

He signed on for 12 years and, as a career soldier, knew that to get promotion through the ranks he needed all three army certificates of education. He passed the third class certificate within two months of joining the Manchesters and the second class just over a year later. This combined with other courses and exemplary behaviour was enough to get him promotion to Colour Sergeant. He received his first award of extra pay and badge for good behaviour in 1903. By this time he had joined his battalion in South Africa, where the Manchesters were on garrison duty following the end of the Boer War. During his time there he passed a Mounted Infantry course.

He was promoted to Lance Corporal in 1904 and Corporal in 1906, and although he reverted to Private at his own request a year later, within a year he was back up to Corporal again. During a couple of months in England in 1907 he qualified as a Physical Training Instructor. The next normal step up would have been as Sergeant Instructor. However, in 1908 the British Army in Great Britain (excluding Ireland) was reorganised and the Territorial Army was established. As a direct consequence Corporal Wilson's battalion in the Manchesters was disbanded and Hugh decided to transfer into the 1st Battalion Royal Irish Fusiliers.

In the Faughs he was based in Palace Barracks near Belfast, then Shorncliffe near Dover. He qualified as a marksman and was promoted as a Sergeant Instructor with the Lewis light machine gun. In 1914 he qualified as a Battalion Shot. All his years of studying and hard work paid off when he was given his first posting on 24 July 1914 as a Sergeant Instructor at the North Wales Infantry Brigade, teaching the Territorials how to fire a machine gun.

He embarked with the British Expeditionary Force in August 1914 and fought during the first battle of the war at Le Cateau, where for his bravery under very heavy fire he was awarded the Medaille Militaire. On 8 October 1914 for his gallantry in the retreat from Mons he was Mentioned in Sir John French's Despatches. He was shot in the leg on 25 April 1915 on the slope outside the heavily fortified village of St Julien as part of the Second Battle of Ypres, close to where Pte Robert Morrow VC was killed.

While was recovering from his wounds in an English hospital he wrote his Journal of the first eight months of the war. After six operations he was discharged from the army as no longer fit for active service. He settled down, married and raised his family in 34 Pembroke Avenue, Patricroft, near Old Trafford football ground in Manchester. However, he had difficulty finding work as the injury to his leg and subsequent operations had left him with a shortened and extremely painful leg, and restricted mobility. He died in 1947, aged only 62 years.

Sgt Hugh Alexander Wilson

Appendix 2
Private Robert Morrow VC

The son of Hugh and Margaret Morrow, Robert was born and raised on a farm near Newmills, Dungannon. At the age of 20 in 1911 he joined the 1st Battalion Royal Irish Fusiliers at Armagh and, after basic training, went with the Battalion to England. In August 1914 the Battalion was ordered to join the British Expeditionary Force, then embarking for France.

Robert was small in stature and a quiet, disciplined, hard-working soldier – he did not look like the stereotypical hero. However, one of his typical exploits happened when he and his friends were in the trenches, only yards away from German snipers. Everyone was very thirsty and to get water meant crossing open ground in clear view of the snipers.

One of his comrades described what happened next:

> 'Robert Morrow was an Irishman who literally did not know the meaning of fear. One day we badly wanted some water, and this was to be had only from a farm some distance away. To reach the farm it was necessary to leave the trenches and cross open ground exposed to the German fire, which was very deadly because we were so near the enemy's trenches. These were only about 600 yards away, and not more than 300 yards from us were some snipers in a farm in front of the trenches. Morrow volunteered to fetch water, and taking an empty two-gallon stone rum jar, he started on his perilous journey.
>
> As soon as he was seen after leaving the trench the Germans did their very best to pot him, but they missed every time, and Morrow reached the farm, filled his jar, and began the trip back. And a hard business it was, for a jar like that will hold about fifty pounds weight of water; then there is the jar, and the awkwardness of carrying it, when the carrier has to duck and dodge every yard of the ground. But Morrow was a splendid hand at the game, and he actually managed to reach the trench in safety, and was on the point of dropping into it with his precious water, and we were just ready to give him a wild Irish cheer, but at this moment crash came a German bullet, and the rum jar was smashed to pieces, and the water rained on the ground and was lost.'
>
> Morrow was the sort of chap who can't be beaten. Instantly he volunteered to go back to his farm with water bottles. This time he reached the trench safely, and dropped into it, bringing the water with him, and escaping every German bullet that was meant to kill him. He was a plucky kid, and we were proud of him, and the Regiment will be proud of him for all time; I say will be, for, like quite a number of the heroes who have won the Cross, Morrow has been killed.'

On 12 April 1915 members of the 1st Battalion were in trenches below Messines Hill when Pte Morrow's company lines came under heavy and accurate shell fire, burying several of the soldiers when the trenches collapsed. Ignoring the shells landing round him, Pte Morrow dug six soldiers out and carried them to safety, returning each time to see who else he could help. For this outstanding act of bravery his name was put forward for a Victoria Cross. He wrote home to tell his family about being put forward for Britain's highest award for bravery, but never received the medal himself. Less than two weeks later he was badly wounded trying to capture St Julien during the Second Battle of Ypres. He died of his wounds the following day, 26 April 1915. His grave is in White House Cemetery near Ypres.

The citation for the Victoria Cross reads: 'For most conspicuous bravery near Messines on 12th April 1915, when he rescued and carried to safety several men who had been buried in the debris of trenches wrecked by shell fire. Pte Morrow carried out this gallant work on his own initiative and under very heavy fire from the enemy.'

His Company Commander, Col G. V. W. Hill DSO, said of him:

> 'It was due to his work and astounding bravery that the company's casualties were not trebled. Morrow was a small unostentatious man, almost a boy, whom one would never imagine as doing outstanding things, yet under fire he was one of those who did not know what fear was. His bravery was the talk of the Company, but unfortunately he never knew he had won the Victoria Cross, for he was wounded near St Julien on 25th April 1915 and died shortly after. It was early in May that we heard he had been awarded the VC.'

King George V presented the Victoria Cross to his mother at Buckingham Palace. Nicholas, Tsar of all the Russias, also awarded Pte Morrow VC the Medal of St George Third Class, for his selfless act of bravery. After the war was over the Regiment raised more than £100 to give to the Morrow family, to enable them to buy the family farm. Knowing the high esteem in which her son had been held, she presented the Victoria Cross to the Regiment in his memory, and his medals are on permanent display in the Royal Irish Fusiliers Museum.

Private Robert Morrow VC

APPENDIX 3
THE LEGEND OF THE ANGEL OF MONS

The legend of the 'Angels of Mons' has existed for 90 years, yet there is no official evidence to support the stories. In the various archives of the British Army there is no proof of any supernatural intervention during the retreat from Mons in August 1914.

Over the years there have been many stories and theories and it would seem that there are still a number of people who firmly believe that divine intervention by an angelic host saved the British Army from destruction when they were fighting a desperate rearguard action against colossal odds.

Did the 'Angels' give sustenance to the British or terrify the enemy? The one fact not in dispute is that on 23 August and again on 26 August 1914 the Germans were abruptly checked in their advance and recoiled in some disorder, allowing the remnant of the British forces to continue their retreat. From that time rumours have constantly circulated regarding the strange incidents that occurred between 23 and 26 August 1914, but just what did happen on those hot summer days in 1914?

In his book *Angels A to Z* Matthew Bunson recounts, 'One of the most famous episodes of angelic intervention [was] the supposedly widely reported descent of an angelic army in August 1914, which came to the aid of the British forces against the Germans in Mons... The angelic host's assistance could not have come at a more propitious moment as the British were being driven back by the relentless German advance.'

One version, apparently verified by German prisoners, described a band of ghost-like archers led by a tall figure on a shining white horse that led the British during an assault on German trenches. Another story told of three angelic beings that were seen by the British Army, hovering in the air over German lines, and providing a source of deep inspiration for them. Added to this were stories that soldiers claimed to have also seen St Michael the Archangel, the Virgin Mary and even Joan of Arc.

None of the eyewitnesses, who asserted that they had viewed the Angel, came forward to have their names recorded in any log or document. British Army veterans who later told of seeing the Angel were suspect and, more importantly, few who fought at Mons survived the war. One who did was John Ewings from Co Tyrone, who was at that time a 35-year-old Private with the 2nd Battalion of the Royal Inniskilling Fusiliers. In 1980, just after his 101st birthday, Ewing gave an interview to BBC Radio in which he described how an angel had saved his life (David Clarke, 'The Angel of Mons', 2004).

One would think that had some sensational vision been witnessed by the men of a particular battalion or company it would be recorded somewhere. In the histories of the regiments involved in the fighting at Mons there is no mention of any events that could be construed as a distraction or intervention during the action. The units that suffered the most casualties on 23 August, the 4th Royal Fusiliers and the 4th Middlesex, did not record any peculiar events whatsoever. Nor did other regiments active in the battle or retreat, such as the Royal West Kents and the 2nd King's Own Scottish Borderers, record anything but the trials and tribulations of the battle.

Nevertheless, something happened around this date to cause many men to put pen to paper in letters, diaries and journals. The British press soon took up these writings, and by 1915 the public accepted that an anomalous event had occurred during the battle and retreat from Mons.

It would appear that the nature of the apparition was angelic rather than saintly or spectral. As a result of this, those in the trenches and their families at home came to believe in a stereotyped legend of the 'Angel of Mons' whose timely appearance showed that God was providing support for the opponents of the Kaiser's hordes, something that was encouraged by both government and church.

Over the years little has changed and historians who have studied Mons have incorporated the legend of the 'Angel of Mons' into their writings up to the present day. Trevor Wilson and Martin Gilbert mention the phantom in their works. Daniel David, in his book *The 1914 Campaign*, states, 'Some beleaguered soldiers reported being rescued by angels and ghostly bowmen'.

Arch Whitehouse mentions in an earlier work, *Heroes and Legends of World War One*, that after the battle a detachment of the Coldstream Guards, being the last to withdraw, lost their way in the Mormal Forest. They had dug-in to make a last stand when an angel appeared as a dimly outlined female figure. She was described as tall and slim, wearing a white flowing gown. The Guardsmen followed the glowing figure across an open field to a hidden, sunken road and made their escape. No explanation is given as to why the Guardsmen should follow such a figure; perhaps they had not seen a woman for a while!

Lynn MacDonald's seminal work, *1914*, includes an account by Captain Arthur Osbon of the 4th Dragoon Guards, a cavalry unit that was involved in the retreat from Mons. He thought that the threatening Cimmerian skies reminded him of Milton's description of legions of dark angels driven by St Michael to the plains of Hell – vividly descriptive, but hardly relevant to succouring angels.

Either something unusual happened during the battle, or in the subsequent retreat, or the legend has a source divorced from the battlefield. The 'Angel of Mons' remains elusive. Eighty years of historical and scientific investigation have left a situation where many reputable sources point to events at Mons, while others treat the Angel as a phenomenon created on the home front.

At that time a typical late August morning started out with mist and rain, but this cleared around 10am to give fair weather with a prevailing westerly wind. There was a warm August sun later in the day, an Ascoli, a stifling August heat and hot sunshine. No weather report mentions unusual cloud formations.

The Royal Flying Corps was active over the battlefield scouting for the enemy and searching for German artillery batteries. The men who comprised the BEF, although unaccustomed to military aircraft, would be unlikely to confuse aircraft or their vapour trails with ethereal phantoms. There are many War Diary entries that confirm that the sight of friendly aircraft raised the morale of the troops on the ground.

It has been suggested that during the hours of darkness the Germans used an airship equipped with powerful searchlights. It is feasible that this could have been confused with an angelic host, but none of the later supposed sightings make reference to an event during the hours of darkness.

As 23 August was a Sunday, was it possible that the idea of forthcoming help had been born during a church service held that morning? Church bells were ringing early and the inhabitants of the villages near the canal were seen in their best attire going to worship. But none of the British unit histories mentions a church parade by the troops at Mons. There is much detail about rations, accommodation and uniform state, but there is no mention of worship during the day.

On 26 August Smith-Dorrien's Second Corps, cut off from Haig's Corps, chose to fight a rear-guard action at Le Cateau. In this action the exhausted soldiers of Dorrien's Corps inflicted heavy casualties on the German First Army and still managed to escape. Despite Le Cateau being fought on the anniversary of the Battle of Crécy, where victory was won by English archers, no link has ever been made with 'angels'.

In September 1914 the writer Arthur Machen published a short story called 'The Bowmen'. This was a fictional account of a phantom English Army led by St George marching from Agincourt to relieve their modern counterparts on an unidentified battlefield. 'The Bowmen' was published in September 1914 in the *London Evening News*. Machen was an author of mildly supernatural stories and a sometime member of a society known as 'The Hermetic Order of the Golden Dawn'. A quote from Machen states: 'The snowball of rumour was set rolling until it was swollen to a monstrous size.'

Machen claimed that, 'In the popular view shining and benevolent supernatural beings are angels. I believe the Bowmen of my story have become "the Angels of Mons".'

An apple orchard near Selvigny. During the retreat from Mons the starving soldiers ate apples from these orchards and sought shelter under their leafy branches.

Unfortunately for Machen his story was published after the supposed happenings in Belgium, so was Machen influenced by the rumours coming from France?

Since the end of the Great War the legend has continued to fester in the minds of both the public and historians, and numerous explanations have been offered from both British and German sources.

In February 1930 the following appeared in a New York newspaper. Colonel Friedrich Herzenwirth, who was described as a former member of the Imperial German Intelligence Service, explained that 'angels' really had appeared at Mons. Apparently German aircraft equipped with enormously powerful cinema projectors had used the clouds as a giant screen. The concept was to create panic among the British troops, but had instead created the opposite effect. Counter propaganda in its purest form! Subsequent investigation proved that both the officer and idea were nothing more than a hoax.

So what was the reason for the heroic stand that stopped the Germans in their tracks on that day? Medical evidence would seem to offer the most logical answer.

The British Army was in retreat, men marched along roads that were different in construction from those they were used to in Britain, and excessive weariness was caused. The distances marched were long, starting at first light and continuing on into the evening, the march quite often interrupted by shelling or the need to fight a rearguard action. There was little food and water was scarce. During the night little shelter was to be found and troops were forced to sleep outdoors with only their groundsheets and greatcoats for shelter. To alleviate this hunger the troops ate apples and pears from the numerous roadside orchards.

So we have a combination of extreme exhaustion, immense stress from combat, dehydration and hunger, the latter assuaged by fresh fruit from the orchards. This fruit not only slaked hunger and thirst, but also provided the body with an energy boost from the natural sugar content.

The evidence for the appearance of angels points to a dire shortage of food, water and rest prior to 23

August and during the subsequent days. From Sgt Wilson's journal we know that they were able to eat enough fruit to appease their hunger and gain a little energy for battle the following day. With regard to 'angels', extreme exhaustion will cause hallucinations, that state where a person suffers errors in perception afflicting some sense organ to such an extent that the person imagines they perceive something for which there is no foundation. For example, a person may fancy he hears himself called during perfect stillness, or may see lights in pitch darkness. Illusions are misinterpreted sensations; for example, the person may constantly mistake articles of furniture for figures of a friend or animal. Both errors occur in sane people and may indicate some slight brain derangement, due to sleeplessness, overwork, feverishness or other cause.

During this chaotic period in late August 1914 it would only take one man to say he had seen an 'angel' or 'angels' to have the story spread like wildfire among men who were in a similar mental state. These were soldiers who were in dire need of something to bolster their flagging morale. With the BEF in retreat, and the situation as desperate as it was, this 'grasping at a straw' was the only alternative to defeat, and who else but an 'angel' would come to the aid of a Christian army?

Appendix 4 Order of Battle of the British Expeditionary Force, August 1914

Commander-in-Chief of the British Forces
Field Marshal Sir J. D. P. French GCB GCVO KCMG
Chief of the General Staff
Lieutenant General Sir A. J. Murray KCB CVO DSO
Adjutant-General
Major General Sir C. F. N. Macready KCB
Quartermaster-General
Major-General W. R. Robertson KCVO CB DSO

Cavalry Division

General Officer Commanding:
Major General E. H. H. Allenby CB
1st Cavalry Brigade
General Officer Commanding:
Brigadier General C. J. Briggs CB
2nd Dragoon Guards
5th Dragoon Guards
11th Hussars
1st Signal Troop
2nd Cavalry Brigade
General Officer Commanding:
Brigadier General H. de B. De Lisle CB DSO
4th Dragoon Guards
9th Lancers
18th Hussars
2nd Signal Troop
3rd Cavalry Brigade
General Officer Commanding:
Brigadier General H. de la Poer Gough CB
4th Hussars
5th Lancers
16th Lancers
3rd Signal Troop
4th Cavalry Brigade
General Officer Commanding:
Brigadier General Hon C. E. Bingham CVO CB
Composite Regiment of Household Cavalry
6th Dragoon Guards
3rd Hussars
4th Signal Troop
5th Cavalry Brigade
General Officer Commanding:
Brigadier General Sir P. W. Chetwode DSO
2nd Dragoons
12th Lancers
20th Hussars

Cavalry Divisional Troops

Royal Horse Artillery
'D', 'E', 'I', 'J' and 'L' Batteries
Royal Engineers
1st Field Squadron
Signal Service
1st Signal Squadron
Army Service Corps
HQ 1st Cavalry Divisional ASC
Medical Units
1st, 2nd, 3rd, 4th and 5th Cavalry Field Ambulances

First Army Corps

Commander-in-Chief
Lieutenant General Sir Douglas Haig KCB KCIE KCVO ADC-Gen

1st Division

General Officer Commanding:
Major General S. H. Lomax
1st Guards Brigade
General Officer Commanding:
Brigadier General F. I. Maxse CVO CB DSO
1st Battalion Coldstream Guards
1st Battalion Scots Guards
1st Battalion Black Watch
2nd Battalion Royal Munster Fusiliers

2nd Infantry Brigade
General Officer Commanding:
Brigadier General E. S. Bulfin CVO CB
2nd Battalion Royal Sussex Regiment
1st Battalion Loyal North Lancashire Regiment
1st Battalion Northamptonshire Regiment
2nd Battalion King's Royal Rifle Corps

3rd Infantry Brigade
General Officer Commanding:
Brigadier General H. J. S. Landon CB
1st Battalion Queen's Royal West Surrey Regiment
1st Battalion South Wales Borderers
1st Battalion Gloucester Regiment
2nd Battalion The Welsh Regiment

Divisional Troops

Mounted Troops
'A' Squadron 15th Hussars
1st Cyclist Company

Artillery
46th, 51st, 54th, 113th, 114th, 115th, 116th, 117th and 118th Royal Field Artillery Batteries
30th, 40th and 57th Howitzer Batteries
26th Heavy Battery Royal Garrison Artillery
1st Division Ammunition Column

Royal Engineers
23rd and 26th Field Companies

Signal Service
1st Signal Company

Army Service Corps
1st Divisional Train

Medical Units
1st, 2nd and 3rd Field Ambulances

In September 1914 the 1st Bn Queen's Own Cameron Highlanders replaced the 2nd Bn Royal Munster Fusiliers in the 1st Guards Brigade.
An Anti-Aircraft Detachment of 1-pounder Pom-Poms was added to the Artillery of all the Divisions in September 1914.

2nd Division

General Officer Commanding:
Major General C. C. Monro CB

4th Guards Brigade
General Officer Commanding:
Brigadier General R. Scott-Kerr CB MVO DSO
2nd Battalion Grenadier Guards
2nd Battalion Coldstream Guards
3rd Battalion Coldstream Guards
1st Battalion Irish Guards

5th Infantry Brigade
General Officer Commanding:
Brigadier General R. C. B. Haking CB
2nd Battalion Worcestershire Regiment
2nd Battalion Oxfordshire & Buckinghamshire Light Infantry
2nd Battalion Highland Light Infantry
2nd Battalion Connaught Rangers

6th Infantry Brigade
General Officer Commanding:
Brigadier General R. H. Davies CB
1st Battalion King's Liverpool Regiment
2nd Battalion South Staffordshire Regiment
1st Battalion Royal Berkshire Regiment
1st Battalion King's Royal Rifle Corps

Divisional Troops

Mounted Troops
'B' Squadron 15th Hussars
2nd Cyclist Company

Royal Artillery
9th, 16th, 17th, 22nd, 50th, 70th, 15th, 48th and 71st Royal Field Artillery Batteries
47th, 56th, and 60th Howitzer Batteries
35th Heavy Battery Royal Garrison Artillery
2nd Division Ammunition Column

Royal Engineers
5th and 11th Field Companies

Second Army Corps

General Officer Commanding:
General Sir H. L. Smith-Dorrien GCB DSO

3rd Division

General Officer Commanding:
Major General H. I. W. Hamilton CVO CB DSO

7th Infantry Brigade
General Officer Commanding:
Brigadier General F. W. N. McCracken CB DSO
3rd Battalion Worcestershire Regiment
2nd Battalion South Lancashire Regiment
1st Battalion Wiltshire Regiment
2nd Battalion Royal Irish Rifles

8th Infantry Brigade
General Officer Commanding:
Brigadier General B. J. C. Doran CB
2nd Battalion Royal Scots
4th Battalion Middlesex Regiment
2nd Battalion Royal Irish Regiment
1st Battalion Gordon Highlanders

9th Infantry Brigade
General Officer Commanding:
Brigadier General F. C. Shaw CB
1st Battalion Northumberland Fusiliers
4th Battalion Royal Fusiliers
1st Battalion Lincolnshire Regiment
1st Battalion Royal Scots Fusiliers

Divisional Troops

Mounted Troops
'A' Squadron 15th Hussars
3rd Cyclist Company
Artillery
6th, 23rd, 29th, 41st, 45th, 49th, 107th, 108th and 109th Royal Field Artillery Batteries
128th, 129th and 130th Howitzer Batteries
48th Heavy Battery Royal Garrison Artillery
3rd Division Ammunition Column
Royal Engineers
56th and 57th Field Companies
Signal Service
3rd Signal Company
Army Service Corps
3rd Divisional Train
Medical Units
7th, 8th and 9th Field Ambulances

In September 1914 the 1st Bn Devonshire Regiment replaced the 1st Bn Gordon Highlanders in the 8th Infantry Brigade.

5th Division

General Officer Commanding:
Major General Sir C. Fergusson CB MVO DSO
13th Infantry Brigade
General Officer Commanding:
Brigadier General G. J. Cuthbert CB
2nd Battalion King's Own Scottish Borderers
2nd Battalion Duke of Wellington's West Riding Regiment
1st Battalion Royal West Kent Regiment
2nd Battalion Yorkshire Light Infantry
14th Infantry Brigade
General Officer Commanding:
Brigadier General S. P. Rolt CB
2nd Battalion Suffolk Regiment
1st Battalion East Surrey Regiment
1st Battalion Duke of Cornwall's Light Infantry
2nd Battalion Manchester Regiment

15th Infantry Brigade
General Officer Commanding:
Brigadier General A. E. W. Count Gleichen KCVO CB CMG DSO
1st Battalion Norfolk Regiment
1st Battalion Bedfordshire Regiment
1st Battalion Cheshire Regiment
1st Battalion Dorsetshire Regiment

Divisional Troops

Mounted Troops
'A' Squadron 19th Hussars
5th Cyclist Company
Artillery
11th, 52nd, 80th, 119th, 120th, 121st, 122nd, 123rd and 124th Royal Field Artillery Batteries
37th, 61st and 65th Howitzer Batteries
108th Heavy Battery Royal Garrison Artillery
5th Divisional Ammunition Column
Royal Engineers
17th and 59th Field Companies
Signal Service
5th Signal Company
Army Service Corps
5th Divisional Train
Medical Units
13th, 14th and 15th Field Ambulances

Third Army Corps

General Officer Commanding:
Major General W. P. Pulteney CB DSO

4th Division

(Landed in France on the night of 22/23 August 1914)
General Officer Commanding:
Major General T. D'O. Snow CB
(known to the soldiers as 'Snow Ball')
10th Infantry Brigade
General Officer Commanding:
Brigadier General J. A. L. Haldane CB DSO
1st Battalion Royal Warwickshire Regiment
2nd Battalion Seaforth Highlanders
1st Battalion Royal Irish Fusiliers
2nd Battalion Royal Dublin Fusiliers
11th Infantry Brigade
General Officer Commanding:
Brigadier General A. G. Hunter-Weston CB DSO
1st Battalion Somerset Light Infantry
1st Battalion East Lancashire Regiment
1st Battalion Hampshire Regiment
1st Battalion Rifle Brigade

12th Infantry Brigade
General Officer Commanding:
Brigadier General H. F. M. Wilson CB
1st Battalion King's Own Royal Lancaster Regiment
2nd Battalion Lancashire Fusiliers
2nd Battalion Royal Inniskilling Fusiliers
2nd Battalion Essex Regiment

Divisional Troops

Mounted Troops
'B' Squadron 19th Hussars
4th Cyclist Company
Artillery
27th, 39th, 68th, 88th, 125th, 126th, 127th, 134th and 135th Royal Field Artillery Batteries
31st, 35th and 55th Howitzer Batteries
31st Heavy Battery Royal Garrison Artillery
4th Divisional Ammunition Column
Royal Engineers
7th and 9th Field Companies
Signal Service
4th Signal Company
Army Service Corps
4th Divisional Train
Medical Units
10th, 11th and 12th Field Ambulances

6th Division

(Embarked for St Nazaire 8/9 September 1914)
General Officer Commanding:
Major General J. L. Keir CB
16th Infantry Brigade
General Officer Commanding:
Brigadier General E. C. Ingouville-Williams CB DSO
(known to the soldiers as 'Inky Bill')
1st Battalion The Buffs East Kent Regiment
1st Battalion Leicestershire Regiment
1st Battalion King's Shropshire Light Infantry
2nd Battalion York & Lancaster Regiment
17th Infantry Brigade
General Officer Commanding:
Brigadier General W. R. B. Doran CB DSO
1st Battalion Royal Fusiliers
1st Battalion Prince of Wales's
North Staffordshire Regiment
2nd Battalion Prince of Wales's Leinster Regiment
3rd Battalion Rifle Brigade
18th Infantry Brigade
General Officer Commanding:
Brigadier General W. N. Congreve VC CB MVO
1st Battalion Prince of Wales's Own
West Yorkshire Regiment
1st Battalion East Yorkshire Regiment
2nd Battalion Sherwood Foresters
2nd Battalion Durham Light Infantry

Divisional Troops

Mounted Troops
'C' Squadron 19th Hussars
6th Cyclist Company
Artillery
21st, 24th, 34th, 42nd, 53rd, 72nd, 110th, 111th and 112th Royal Field Artillery Batteries
43rd, 86th and 87th Howitzer Batteries
24th Heavy Battery Royal Garrison Artillery
6th Divisional Ammunition Column
Royal Engineers
12th and 38th Field Companies
Signal Service
6th Signal Company
Army Service Corps
6th Divisional Train
Medical Units
16th, 17th and 18th Field Ambulances

Army Troops

Mounted Troops
'A' and 'C' Squadrons North Irish Horse
'B' Squadron South Irish Horse
Medium Siege Artillery
1st, 2nd, 3rd, 4th, 5th, and 6th Siege Batteries
Royal Garrison Artillery
Royal Engineers
HQ of GHQ 1st, 2nd and 3rd Signal Companies
A to E Air-line Sections
F to P Cable Sections
Q Wireless Section

Royal Flying Corps

Commander:
Brigadier General Sir D. Henderson KCB DSO
2nd, 3rd, 4th, 5th and 6th Aeroplane Squadrons
Infantry
1st Battalion Queen's Own Cameron Highlanders
Army Service Corps
Army Troops Train
Medical Units
19th and 20th Field Ambulances
Lines of Communication Defence Troops
1st Battalion Devonshire Regiment

2nd Battalion Royal Welch Fusiliers
1st Battalion Cameronians
1st Battalion Duke of Cambridge's
Own Middlesex Regiment
2nd Battalion Argyll & Sutherland Highlanders
These four battalions were formed into the 19th Infantry Brigade at Valenciennes on 22 August 1914 under the command of Major General L. G. Drummond CB MVO

Lines of Communication Units

Royal Engineers
Railway Transport Establishment
8th and 10th Railway Companies
29th Works Company
10th and 42nd Fortress Companies
1st Printing Company
Royal Flying Corps
1st Aircraft Park
Signal Service
1st Signal Company
Army Service Corps
Cavalry Ammunition Park
5th Cavalry Brigade Ammunition Park
1st to 6th Divisional Ammunition Parks
Cavalry Supply Column
5th Cavalry Brigade Supply Column
1st to 6th Divisional Supply Columns
Army Troops Supply Column
Base Mechanical Transport Depot
Advanced Mechanical Transport Depot
Base Horse Transport Depot
Advanced Horse Transport Depot
1st to 6th Reserve Parks (two-horsed wagons)
1st to 6th Field Butcheries
1st to 6th Field Bakeries
1st to 8th Railway Supply Detachments
Central Requisition Office
Branch Requisition Office
1st to 30th Deport Units of Supply
1st to 8th Bakery Sections
Nos 1 and 2 Advanced Remount Depots
Base Remount Depot
Medical Units
1st to 6th Clearing Hospitals
1st to 12th Stationary Hospitals
1st to 12th General Hospitals
1st to 6th Ambulance Trains
Nos 1, 2 and 3 Hospital Ships
1st to 3rd Advanced Depots of Medical Stores
1st to 3rd Base Depots of Medical Stores
1st and 2nd Sanitary Sections
1st to 11th Sanitary Squads
Convalescent Depot
Ordnance Units
1st to 8th Ordnance Companies
Veterinary Units
1st to 7th Mobile Veterinary Sections (8th to 11th Sections followed later)
1st to 8th Veterinary Sections
Base Depot of Veterinary Stores
Army Pay Unit
Base Army Pay Department Unit
Postal Units
Base Post Office
Advance Post Office
1st and 2nd Stationary Post Offices
Prisons
Military Prisons in the Field
Bases
Nos 1, 2 and 3 Bases

INDEX